THE IBO

FIELD GUIDE

INSPIRED BY
L EADERS OF THE FIELD

ISBN 0-9722332-5-3
Published by MotiVision Media
This is the first edition September 2006

Content Editor and Writer–Naomi Goegan
Cover Design–MotiVision Media
Layout and Graphics–MotiVision Media

Special thanks to the countless Diamonds and above for their direct and/or indirect contribution to this project. In order that the information contained in this book may be available to all organizations, the publisher has chosen to use fictional names in place of actual names.

Contents

Intro

List

Invite

STP

F-T

Lead

Q&A

READ ME FIRST

The IBO Field Guide is a compilation of the skills and techniques applied by top achievers in the Quixtar® business. No one author can take credit for the information in this book; it is a melding of what has been learned and shared for years by countless leaders within our industry. Whether you are brand new in the business or a seasoned IBO, you will find straightforward, no-nonsense solutions in this guide to help you build your business.

While this book focuses primarily on improving your skill level, no amount of skill can compensate for ineffective thinking. So in addition to reading through The IBO Field Guide, get involved in your team's continuing education program. And as often as possible, associate with team members who are more experienced than you because the fastest way to become a champion is to hang around one.

In a business of duplication, the slightest change can have great impact. Every thing you do, not only trickles down into your own group, but also has the potential to affect everyone else's business around you. It is vital that if any of the information in this book differs from your support team's teachings, you disregard the information altogether or discuss it with your support team before making any changes.

Remember the movie The Karate Kid? The young boy, Daniel, anxious to learn Karate, finally finds a mentor. On his first day of training he doesn't receive typical Karate instruction. Miyagi, his sensei, has him perform laborious chores like waxing his car, sanding the deck, and painting his fence. Daniel is puzzled and impatient with Miyagi because he wants to learn Karate! Then one day, Daniel gets into a sparring match and Miyagi tells him, "Wax on!" And he instinctively blocks the hit. "Wax off!" He blocks another. In that moment, Daniel realizes there was a method to his mentor's teachings. There was a purpose in doing all those chores with those movements; he was in fact subconsciously learning to become a master of his trade.

Just like Daniel, much of the training in this book and in the business may not make sense to you at first. You might think it pointless to do things the way your coaches recommend. But as you progress in building your business, it will all begin to click into place and make sense. Rest assured that your business partners do not want to see you get beaten to a pulp! They are trying to teach you the proven patterns of building this business so you can succeed.

To get the most out of your copy of The IBO Field Guide, highlight, underline, dog ear, take notes, rewrite, practice, memorize, apply, refresh, revisit, and thoroughly get acquainted with these skills until they become a part of you. Applying what you learn, as you learn, ensures retention and also helps your skills to develop at an accelerated rate. When you successfully absorb this information and use it in the field on a consistent basis, you'll find yourself building bigger, better organizations, faster and easier than ever before.

INTRODUCTION

Economic projections and experts tell us that 10 million millionaires will be created in the next 10 years. In fact, world famous economist, Paul Zane Pilzer, says that a majority of those millionaires will be created in the direct selling industry. He states that our economy is poised for a growth spurt that is set to dwarf the explosion of the 1990s, and that those entering home managed businesses driven by the efficiencies of the web are perfectly positioned to benefit from the boom ahead.

10 million millionaires. Will you be one of them?

If you are like most IBOs, you are already convinced that the on-line shopping trend is the wave of the future and you're fairly effective at convincing others about it. You know your business, you understand its potential, and you know how to explain it to people.

But… are you really getting the results you want? Are you happy with the amount of money you are making? Are you affecting change in people and moving them to productive action?

Convincing people that this business makes sense and getting them to sign a registration form is one thing. Engaging them in the process of pursuing their dreams through this business vehicle is an entirely different level of influence. The good news is that influence can be learned by anyone.

There was a man who came up to me after an open meeting once and said, "Let's be honest, it takes a certain type of person to make this work. Not everyone is going to accomplish what you have." I responded by saying, "You're right. It takes a certain type of person. Someone who is Teachable and Motivated."

In other words, a person has to have a reason for building the business and he has to be open to learning how to build it. No one is born with genes predisposing them for success; those abilities are acquired through learning and experience. You possess all the "equipment" you need to lead in the field - and if you dare, you will build this business and live your dream.

Figure it out for yourself, my lad,
You have all that the greatest of men have had,
Two arms, two hands, two legs, two eyes
And a brain to use if you would be wise.
With this equipment they all began,
So start for the top and say, "I can."

Look them over, the wise and great.
They take their food from a common plate,
And similar knives and forks they use,
With similar laces they tie their shoes.
The world considers them brave and smart,
But you've all they had when they made their start.

You can triumph and come to skill,
You can be great if you only will.
You're well equipped for what fight you choose,
You have legs and arms and a brain to use,
And the man who has risen great deeds to do
Began his life with no more than you.

You are the handicap you must face,
You are the one who must choose your place,
You must say where you want to go,
How much you will study the truth to know.
God has equipped you for life, but He
Lets you decide what you want to be.

Courage must come from the soul within,
The man must furnish the will to win.
So figure it out for yourself, my lad.
You were born with all that the great have had,
With your equipment they all began,
Get hold of yourself and say: "I can."

-Edgar A. Guest

We wish you all the success you are willing to work for!
–Leaders of the Field

ARE YOU READY TO TAKE THE FIELD?

As a Quixtar® IBO you own a business backed by a corporation whose sales exceed $6.8 billion since its inception in 1999, over $2.2 billion of which was paid back in bonuses and incentives to business owners just like you. Your dot com was ranked as the number one online retailer in the Health & Beauty category, and among the top 15 e-commerce sites overall according to Internet Retailer's Top 400 Guide.

The corporate headquarters handling the back end of your business consists of over 80 separate buildings on 300 acres that span more than 4 million square feet. And your order fulfillment is supported by six distribution centers across North America totaling over 1.5

million square feet that delivers 13.5 million packages a year, 99.7% of which are on time. Customer Support for your business handles 1 million telephone order transactions a year, 90% of which are answered in less than a minute.

Products available exclusively through your business include: the first personalized health program to ever combine genetic testing and nutrigenomic supplements, the number one selling energy drink manufactured in the U.S., a brand of vitamins, minerals, and dietary supplements that outsell any other in the world, and a cosmetic line that is one of the top five largest-selling prestige brands in the world. These and other exclusive products for your business are engineered by over 500 R&D and Quality Assurance scientists and support staff who perform over 500,000 tests annually to ensure consistent quality.

The question isn't whether you have your hands on a viable business or not. The question is: how much of its viability are you ready to capitalize on?

The good news is that it won't require any formal education for you to start making money in your business. Regardless of what you have or have not done in the past or what career choices you may have made, you can achieve the kind of success you dream of.

What your success *will* require is that you learn and apply new information. Let's face it, if you knew how to make the kind of residual income you need to live the lifestyle of your dreams, you would have done it already. So what is there to learn?

Aside from the obvious – the web site, the products, the business plan – learning to manage time, money, and people is integral to success. For the most part we'll be talking about people skills because they are the bedrock of this business. As great as the dot com, the products, and the compensation plan are, it is people who build profitable businesses.

And here's the tricky part: in this business people do not work for you. You have no power to hire or fire people based on their performance nor does anyone need your approval to get a raise or time off. The only influence you have over your prospects, customers, and IBOs is the influence you earn.

So how, without the luxury of authority, do we influence people? This is the sticking point for most IBOs. And it is the difference between failure and success at every level in your business.

PREPARING TO BECOME A FIELD GUIDE

Before we can learn to influence people, we must first understand their nature. And the nature of people is that, for the most part, we make decisions based on how we feel more than we do on logic. If you were told that there is a widget that was x inches long, y inches wide, and z inches in height that weighed 7 lbs., sells for $19.99, that can be delivered to your door by 3 o'clock tomorrow, how excited would you be to buy it? What if instead, a trusted friend told you that this widget has made people happier, healthier, and more successful? You would probably want to know more wouldn't you?

The fact is that trust, relatability, and other emotional factors play a much greater role in business decisions than we might expect. Logically, there's no reason why everyone wouldn't want to ride the greatest socio-economic trend of our time and profit from it in a low-risk business. Our business is a total no-brainer. But not everyone will get involved when you show them the plan and sometimes, it will be because of how they feel about you.

That's no judgment on you. It just means that people are going to filter the opportunity through their perceptions of you — whatever they may be. Perceptions like: Is this person trustworthy? Credible? Confident? Can this person really help me? Does this person really care about me? Do I like this person and want to be around her? The way people feel about you is equally as important as how they feel about the business itself, if not more so.

If you don't feel confident and capable right now, that's okay. Don't beat yourself up about it. You're in good company. Most, if not all of the top achievers in this business were at one time socially and/or professionally "challenged" in some way. There are those who stuttered, those who didn't like people, those who people didn't like, others with past failures, low self esteem – you name it. But in spite of it all, they developed a high level of confidence and influenced thousands of people.

How did they do it? Where did their confidence come from? They must have lucked into getting great results, which in turn bolstered their confidence and ability to influence. Let's take a look at a couple of real life stories from the field to see whether it really was "luck" that did it for them:

Lane and his wife Kathy were intent on building their business after losing hope in Lane's career. In their first year of business, they showed the plan practically every night. And at the end of that year, their entire business sat at 1000 points. Disappointing? For most people, yes; but Lane and Kathy kept going. They showed the plan consistently for another full year. And at the end of two years, their total group volume was at 4000 PV. If you had these results, would you have quit? At the end of their third year in business, they finally hit 7500 PV.

Before we tell you what happened to Lane and Kathy, let's take a look at Robert and Cindy's story. Robert and Cindy had hit 7500 points after two years in the business, but their volume had fallen back down. According to Robert, they were frustrated.

We'd show 15 plans, look at the results, and I'd think, "What am I doing wrong?" Then we'd show another 15 plans and look at the results again. We gained one, lost two, gained two, lost three; and the ones we gained I wish we hadn't! I kept thinking, "What's wrong with me? What's wrong with me? What's wrong with me?"

Then Robert heard from someone in the business that if he were to show 300 plans without doubting, he would be an Emerald. Frustrated with his results, he decided to commit to it. After his first 100 plans, he had zero people who stuck in his business. Very disappointing, but he had committed to 300 so he kept going. After his second 100 plans, he had somewhere around twenty people who stuck in his business. He still didn't have the results he wanted. But he was committed to 300 so he kept going.

If these stories were to end there, would they look similar to your own story up until this point? Let's take a look at what happened from there.

Lane and Kathy went diamond two years after hitting 7500 points in their business. Robert and Cindy, at the time they finished their 300th plan, were in their second month of Emerald qualification.

So back to our earlier point: Did their confidence come from their results? Was it a lucky break? No. **Confidence is a result of knowing who you are and where you are going. It is a result of disciplined action.** As long as your confidence rests on your ability to produce results, you will ride the roller coaster up and down and up and back down again. You must know where you stand – especially when there are absolutely no results to show for.

Take it or leave it, for most leaders, knowing who they are is a spiritual matter. In times of doubt, they lean on the knowledge that they were created with purpose, and no fear, circumstance, or adversity can come against their fulfillment of it.

And somewhere along the line, they hit a tipping point where disciplined action bred confidence within them. An internal change occurred and they stopped asking "What's wrong with me?" Instead, they stood firm on their beliefs and started asking, "What's wrong with them? If they're not seeing this then they aren't right for my business." They developed confidence and declared, "NEXT!"

Terry and Pam struggled five and a half years to hit Gold Producer. One year later they were Emeralds and another year after that, Diamonds. Steve and Mary, after six years in the business had a group volume of 2000 PV. Three years later they were Diamonds. Story after story we see leaders who remained disciplined in their activity hit a tipping point where their results skyrocketed.

Were those years without tangible results wasted or were they worthwhile? It was during that time that those leaders were being prepared for the fantastic growth to come. It's where they developed the fight to conquer anything that stood in the way of victory.

Here is a list of some additional things that Lane and Kathy, Robert and Cindy, and other leaders in the field have done to build their confidence.

Build your dream. It all starts with a dream. It's the "why" behind the "how". Try this exercise: take a look at the back of your hands. Focus on them for a minute. Now close your eyes and imagine your hands wrapped around the steering wheel of your dream car. Picture yourself driving it. Revel in the emotion you feel as you experience that car. You can do the same with any dream you have, tangible or not. Picture the expression on someone's face or the sense of anticipation as you hand someone a special gift; whatever your dream, imagine living it and savor the good feelings it produces in you.

Our thoughts have a profound impact on what manifests into our lives. The more we focus on what we want, the more we attract that into our lives. By the same token, the more we focus on what we don't want, the worse we feel, the worse we perform, and consequently, the more we attract what we don't want.

Dress sharp. No need to give up your style while you conduct business (unless it's sloppy, sleazy, or downright scary), but do dress up to the same level of professionalism as your leaders. Professionally dressed people draw more trust, respect, and credibility. If you need some help picking out the right threads, or if you have questions about hair, make-up, to shave or not to shave, etc., get some perspective from someone on your support team.

Smile and be yourself. People who smile are 100% more approachable. Smiling is also the quickest, least expensive way to improve your looks and your results in the business. You are at your best when you are true to your inner self. Don't try to be something or someone that you aren't; just work on being the best you.

Get organized. Don't clutter your valuable mind space with things you need to remember. As a professional in this business you need your brain to think. Get yourself a pocket calendar, a notebook, or a planner and write everything down. Important dates, tasks, your prospect list, your dreams, goals, thoughts - write it all down. The more you dump your thoughts on paper, the more space you'll have in your brain to think. Try it and you'll be amazed at how the fog lifts!

Prepare to do business. Have on hand what you need to show the business plan and to follow through with prospects including any first night materials you may want to leave them. You should also have your own set of personal favorites (books/audios) to keep you up and on your game, especially after those times when your prospect turns out to be a dud. Don't load up on a bunch of stuff you're never going to use, but don't shortchange the things that you do need.

Know and use your products. It's the building block of our business. The plan doesn't work unless products are moving through an organization. Set up your Ditto Scheduled Order™ and start using your own products.

Start reading, listening, and learning.
Give yourself a week before your attitude is challenged. The only way to equip yourself with the right answers, the right attitude, and the right perspective for what you are about to face as you talk to people about your business is to devour the books and audios recommended by your coach. Your support team has some sort of a continuing education program they recommend - subscribe to it. Whether you are smart or not, when you read and listen often, you'll come across as an informed business owner because you've acquired the knowledge, attitude, and belief of top leaders. And even if you feel you don't need it, there will be someone on your team who does. Stay informed and you'll know what books and audios to promote to your team.

Set a goal. Point your compass toward something achievable that is also a bit of a stretch. If you don't have a simple goal that comes to your mind this instant, stop reading, give it some thought and then write it down. Talk it over with your support team and develop a strategy to attain it. Short-term goals give you focus, they get you moving, and of course, when accomplished, you'll feel great to have a win under your belt.

Keep an open line of communication. People headed for quicksand usually don't know it so it's important to keep in regular communication with someone on your support team who can guide you through the field you're trekking. One piece of advice could be the difference between one week and one year. Keep them informed of what's going on and try to learn from them every step of the way.

Aside from building our own confidence, we also want to build people's confidence in us. We want to learn to operate in a way that establishes trust and credibility. In his book, *How the Best Get Better*, Dan Sullivan suggests practicing the following **four habits:**

1. Show up on time. When you have an appointment and you show up late, or worse, not at all, you're wasting a person's most valuable commodity: time. That makes them feel really bad about you. Showing up on time is a matter of good planning. Prepare your materials in advance and plan on getting to your appointments a few minutes early. If you are late or unable to make it, have the courtesy to call ahead of time.

2. Do what you say. Remember the story about the boy who cried, "Wolf!" one too many times? He lost credibility and the entire town shunned him - for good reason! When it comes to business, people feel better about doing business with you when what you say comes true. If you're not sure whether you can keep your word or not, don't offer it! It's better to under-promise and over-deliver than to consistently fall short on your word.

3. Finish what you start. If you're in it to go Diamond, go Diamond. And if you tell someone you're going to help them, help them. It's a cop-out to think, "Well… I didn't know they were going to be so stubborn." Or, "Well… my friends didn't get involved like they said they would." People who only do what is easy or what everyone else is doing are difficult to depend on. Don't do the easy thing–do the right thing and finish what you start.

4. Say "Please" and "Thank you." Politeness, or simple courtesy, is often overlooked today. People feel appreciated, respected, and cared for when you are polite to them. Being courteous is one of the easiest ways to separate yourself from the pack. Your prospects will feel better around you and will refer more business your way when you treat them with regard.

DO THE LOOP

There are **five fundamental action steps** to building your business. They are: making a names list, contacting and inviting, showing the business plan, follow through, and repeating the process (duplication). These are the five simple steps you will master. With each of these steps your objective is to learn the step, take action and perform the step, and then turn around and successfully teach that step to others. We learn, do, and teach.

Because of the nature of our business, we sometimes find ourselves having to do before we've had the chance to learn. Or we may find ourselves in a position to teach a new IBO before we're ready. If you find yourself in this situation, don't panic or pretend to be more knowledgeable than you really are. Use your support team; that's what they're there for! It's perfectly okay to let somebody know that you don't have all the answers – just introduce him to an audio, a book, or your senior associate who does have the answers.

With any new skill you are trying to learn, give yourself permission to fail a few times before becoming skilled and natural in applying it. A failed attempt doesn't make you a failure. It makes you better. It's life's way of revealing the important lessons we are to learn. Practice, repetition, and experience always come before expertise so focus initially on quantity. Just get out there and get some experience under your belt first.

Once your level of activity becomes a habit and you gain experience, shift your focus to quality. What do you need to fine-tune to get better results? Are there any negative patterns you're seeing in people's responses that could be avoided? Are you hearing the same excuses over and over? Go back and hit the books and CDs and talk to your support team to see if there's something you've missed or something new that can be learned.

Learning new things can be frustrating at times if we don't keep ourselves in the right perspective. Take your business seriously, but don't take yourself too seriously. Learn to laugh at yourself, have fun, and trust your ability to improve with experience.

THE NAMES LIST

The first action step to building your business is developing your written names list. **Our business is driven by word of mouth, period. No advertising, no commercials, no banner ads, no spam, no flyers; our business grows when one person talks to another person.** That usually happens over the phone, in-person, or occasionally through e-mail or other technologies.

What's unique about our industry is that if you want to reach a million people, you don't have to go out and personally talk to 15,000 people each year for 66 years. Rather, you can develop a team of people who share in the task, benefiting from the results proportionately. A hundred people who each add 10 people, who show the business idea 15 times per month, would reach a million people in 5 ½ years. Get the idea?

So why do we have to write people's names down on paper? As long as they're accessible, why bother? For one, it's always best to keep information out of your brain and on paper so you have room to think. It's also a good way to keep track of who you've called, shown the plan to, left materials with, etc. Remember, we're not planning a social; we're building a business.

Every new IBO who joins your team also needs to be walked through the process of writing out a names list. Why? Because the next potential leader in your group, or someone who may eventually lead you to one, is most likely going to come from their written names list. Why would any IBO in their right mind leave something so significant to chance?

Left to chance, most people never write out a names list. Left to chance, the people who do write out a names list write down less than ten names. Left to chance, those ten names are the least successful people they know. And left to chance, those people won't be teachable or motivated, they won't build the business, and your team will not grow. So set your team up for success by learning, doing, and teaching a written names list.

Helping people make a written names list is a simple task that pays big dividends. Your objective is to have people write down the names of everyone they know. **You're looking for "PHDs" – not the doctor kind – but people who are Poorer than they want, Hungry, and Determined to change their situation.**

Don't prejudge anyone. Sometimes people avoid writing down the names of people who they think already "have it all." Remember that just because someone has everything *you* want doesn't mean that they have everything *they* want. And just because someone doesn't have much doesn't mean that they aren't ambitious. Until a person comes face to face with this business opportunity, there's no telling what they'll actually do.

Anyone who has been on the planet for over 18 years ought to know the names of at least a couple hundred people they could write down on a list. But asking the question, "Who do you know?" usually draws a blank because it's too broad of a realm. Our minds tend to compartmentalize information so it's easier for us to think

of people in categories like: friends, family, work, school, gym/workout, associations, clubs, sports (kids teams), music, networking group, online community, neighbors, church/temple, cultural (ex. Latino). Start by thinking of at least three categories of people and write those categories across the top of a piece of paper.

Here are some additional categories/occupations that may help jog your memory:

Airlines/Travel/Vacation	Home improvement
Teams/Sports/Coaches	Law/Attorney
Sales/Service/Insurance	Baby Sitter/Tutor
Banker/Loans	Construction Trades
Restaurant staff	Dentist/Hygienist
Gym/Trainer/Dietitian	Doctor/Physician
Educator/Teacher/Staff	Fireman/Police/Security
Hair Stylist/Nails/Tan	Housekeeper/Maintenance
Computer/IT/Software	Military
Musician/Music/iPod	UPS/Postal Service
PTA Members/Parents	Church/Pastor/Minister
Realtor/Title	School/Student
Truck/Taxi/Bus Driver	Wedding

Starting with the first category, write down all the names of the people who come to mind. When you draw a blank, move on to the next category, and then the next until there are names filled in for each category. For example, if you wrote down your work or career as a category, people who would fall into this list would include people you work with in your office or establishment of business. You would also include people you come in contact with at work, like employees from other departments, vendors, sales people, account reps, etc.

21

Let's say you work as a food server in a restaurant. People in your "work" category might include:

> Regular patrons
> Other food servers
> People in delivery
> Host staff and Matre'D
> Food and Service vendors
> Marketing/Advertising reps
> Kitchen staff and "bus boys"
> Restaurant or hotel managers

Most of us have some way of compiling contact information for the people we know. The most common is our cell phone. Consider these sources as well: address book, planner, or depending on how tech savvy we are, an e-mail program, PDA, or iPod. We may also have a pre-made list of names from a recent graduation, birthday party, wedding, or family gathering. Access these resources to help put together an initial list.

Write down at least ten names in each category. If you can think of more, keep going, don't stop at just three categories with ten names. When you are finished writing down all the names of the people you know, go back to the first category and look at the names you wrote down. Ask yourself, who is the most influential person in that group? Who has the most credibility with others? Who do people listen to and turn to for advice? Who organizes the get-togethers? Bring that name to the top of the list.

Continue to finesse the rest of the names in that category in order of influence. When you are done with that category, do the same with the rest of the categories on your list. You may also want to prioritize people by location. When first starting your business it is most efficient to start with people who are within an hour's drive.

Your names list will either be an asset or a liability in your business. With little to no names on it, your list is a liability costing you belief, attitude, and posture. With an abundance of names on it, your list is an asset. It adds to your excitement, your belief, and your confidence. It can also be used to motivate new IBOs in your team. When someone knows that she is going to benefit from everything that happens with the other people in her category on your list, it adds to her belief and willingness to become an encouraging team player.

The goal is not simply to have a list, but to get names off the list. Names lists should be dynamic, constantly moving, and changing. Revisit your list often and rewrite it monthly to get rid of any names you've crossed off. The last thing you want when you go to call someone new on your list is to see the names of people who may have already said "No." Don't let your list become an eyesore. Keep it fresh and focused on the future potential of your business.

In the first week after starting his business, Sean called every name in his cell phone and invited them to see the business plan. Every name that is, except the three most successful people he knew. He wanted to establish some results before talking to them about the business because he felt he lacked credibility. That year, Sean worked his tail off trying to make something happen with the people he registered from his initial blast of calls. But very little happened in the way of results and Sean grew frustrated. After hearing a speaker at a weekend conference, he decided to call the three successful people he had hesitated to call before. All three chose to get registered in the business and within 18 months, two of them hit the Platinum level. Sean's other legs watched the new growth and excitement and caught fire too. Sean was a qualified Emerald with four legs the following year.

Adding Names To Your List

People don't quit the business because they can't find enough people to say "yes" to the plan; they quit because they don't have enough people to show the plan to. In other words, they run out of names. But there is no shortage of names, only a shortage of people who have learned how to add names to their list. If you can say "Hi" to someone new, start a conversation, and ask a few questions to determine if they're looking, you can go Diamond in this business because you will never run out of people to show the plan to.

An endless names list = a hopeful, excited IBO.
A dry names list = a needy IBO.

Neediness results in loss of belief and confidence, begging, groveling, frustration, and misdirected anger. Always, always, ALWAYS add to your names list to keep your pipeline full. It also doesn't hurt to show the IBOs in your business how simple it is to add names to their list.

One way to meet new people is to ask for referrals when someone says "no" to the plan. Just like you, the people on your names list also know many people. And whether the people you know are looking for opportunity or not, some of the people they know are. So why not ask for referrals? Let's say you have 200 people on your names list. Even if only a quarter of those people each referred you to one person, that's 50 people! Would it be easier for you to meet 50 new people or to make it a habit of asking for a referral?

So long as you've been courteous and respectful with your prospects, they will be open to giving you referrals. You can ask for referrals by saying, "John & Sue, I can see that we don't have a fit and that's fine. As I mentioned, we're looking to fill this position in the next 2 weeks. Who do you know who might have interest in making an additional $2 – $3,000 a month?" Whether they know someone or not doesn't really matter. What matters is that by asking for referrals consistently you will, at some point, get them.

Now let's talk about getting off the couch and out the door to meet new people. No one will be coming to your door asking to be added to your list so it's important that you get out from your home. Go look at cars, homes, boats, coaches, furniture, TVs, computers, clothes, or even bug spray at Home Depot. It doesn't matter what you're looking at, it's being around people that matters. Say "Yes" to any social gathering you're invited to: weddings, graduations, baptisms, BBQ's, holiday parties, play dates, etc. Attend trade shows, home shows, boat shows, festivals, any other events happening in your area. Go join an association, a gym, or a club. Go everywhere with the intention of talking to people you don't know.

List

If you're sitting around idle, complaining that you don't know anyone, you're opting for failure. Life and people are happening all around you and many of those people are looking for opportunity. When you develop the habit of getting to know people everywhere you go, you'll never have to go out "prospecting." Just get out the door and say "Hi!" And don't just drag yourself around thinking, "Woe is me." Stand tall, smile, walk briskly, exude some energy, and make eye contact. If you don't feel like that's "you," just act as if.

It doesn't matter if you're ugly, beautiful, fat, skinny, short, tall, young, or old. There are plenty of celebrities, sports figures, politicians, and wealthy business owners who fit the same description who have no problem meeting people. What matters is your attitude and approachability. If you don't feel like an influential business owner, act like one and soon enough you will catch up with your act.

To make a great first impression with people, somewhere within the first few minutes of a conversation, smile, stick out your hand, look them in the eye and say, "By the way, I'm _____ (name), and you are…" This simple gesture portrays confidence and professionalism and also shows regard for the other person.

When you shake a person's hand, hold his hand so that the webs of your thumbs are touching and shake twice from the elbow, not the shoulder. A wet noodle or a bone crusher gives off the impression that you really don't have it together. So make it a firm handshake and adjust slightly to match the grip pressure of the other person.

Starting a conversation doesn't take much. **People love to talk about themselves so start with a question or a sincere compliment.** State the obvious: "Nice car, how do you like it?" "Great tie, where'd you get it?" "Late lunch?" "Getting some coffee?" "Are those your kids?" "Rough day?" We're not talking rocket science here. Ending your statements with a question gets the conversation going. If someone is unresponsive or you're getting the vibe that he just doesn't want you to talk to him, take the hint and find someone else who does want to talk.

Some of you may be getting a poor response because you're going straight for the jugular without ever finding out if a person is looking. You're rifling through people saying, "Hi, nice to meet you. What do you do? Great! Hey, do you ever look at ways to make additional income?" Stop. STOP! It's too much too soon. STOP and slow down. You're not out spear chucking prospects.

Prospecting is a numbers game; talk to a lot and you'll find a few. But it's also a matter of being likable, appropriate, and sincere. So first define who your ideal prospect is and then go find those people. Most people who fear meeting new people have probably run into this type of person and are under the impression that they will have to be just as callous to successfully add names to their list. Thankfully, that's a misconception. Anyone can successfully meet new people and if you aren't the "used car salesman" type, that's your first advantage.

When talking to someone new ask him what he does. What made him decide to get into his particular field? Does he enjoy what he does? Then listen. Don't try to create a reason why he should consider looking at a business idea. Let him tell you why he's looking.

For example, if you're talking to someone who owns a traditional business, say, "You must love the freedom of owning your own business." Most often his response will be something along the lines of, "Well, it's not all it's cracked up to be." Instead of chiming in your own opinions at this point, play dumb. "Really? Why's that?" Given the opportunity, he will tell you why he dislikes what he does. You can then ask him what he'd ideally like to be doing.

Once you know that a person is looking and why he's looking, you can ask him if he'd be interested in taking a look at a business idea. If he dislikes being a traditional business owner because he never has time, ask him if he'd be interested in a way to create residual income to free up his time. Present the business to people in terms of what they want and you'll garner more interest.

Be careful not to clump everyone into the wanting "time" or "money" category. Often times people are motivated by something else like: significance, friendship, camaraderie, fun, a new challenge, a way to help others, a product that improves their health, or a service that simplifies their life.

Realize that not everyone is an ideal prospect. You're looking for people who are teachable and motivated; people who have a desire to change or improve something in their life who are willing to work to get what they want. Directing your questions with that in mind, you can determine whether people are looking or not within the first few minutes of conversation. And when they are, you can then comfortably and appropriately ask a question to see if they're open to looking at a business idea (See inviting lines in the next chapter). You'll know you're on the right track when people say, "Tell me more about your business." They may not ever join your team, but you've taken an interest in them and now they're sincerely interested in knowing more about you.

Another great way to introduce people to the business is to lead with a product. A question like, "Do you drink energy drinks?" is a straight lead into a conversation about XS™. "Have you ever heard of customized supplements?" is an easy lead into Gensona™ and Nutrilite™. Once you determine a person's interest in a product, you can ask him if he'd be interested in keeping the profit.

Bottom line, the only person who will waste your time spent in this business is you, not your prospects. You're the one who decides who you will show the plan to. You're the one who decides whether it's worth it to squirt gas in your car and spend a night away from your family to sit across the table and share this idea with someone. If you're not taking the time to "qualify" people (find out if they're looking) before you invite them to see the plan, you have no one to blame but yourself when they turn out to be a "No". Never blame a prospect for not moving forward with the business. Either he or she was never qualified to begin with or you had a weak presentation. Both of those are your fault.

INVITING

The second action step is where we invite people to see the coolest business idea on the planet! It is also referred to as the "contact." This step ramps you up for the main event and has a direct impact on your results in the business so **it's hugely important to develop strong confidence in this area.** Be yourself, have fun, and prepare, prepare, prepare.

Imagine the coach of an NFL team handing each rookie a playbook and saying, "Our first game is against the Patriots. Have all these plays mastered and we'll see you then." That would prove to be a dismal performance. Tell me and I will soon forget. Show me and I may remember. Let me try and I will understand.

Don't leave this crucial step to chance. People will often tell you that they already know what to say, especially when they've had some experience making calls before. Don't take their word for it. If they're really that good at making calls, it'll be apparent in your role-play with them. Our industry has its own nuances that people don't understand so you need to determine their preparedness or else you're setting them up to fail.

To prepare for the invite, start by writing out a script that can be easily followed. Here's an example of a basic script for the invite:

1. **Clear the time.**
   "Am I catching you at a bad time or do you have a second?"

2. **Purpose of the call.**
   "I'm working with a friend of mine who's expanding a business project."

3. Are you looking?

"He/She is looking for a few key people. If the money was right and it fit into your schedule would you be open to looking at a business idea?"

4. Set an appointment.

"What nights this week do you already have commitments?"

5. Confirm the appointment.

"I'm writing this in my calendar, are you writing it in yours?"

Invite

In addition to the script, write out responses to these
three common questions:

"What is it?"
"Can you tell me more about it?"
"I'm too busy, I don't have time."

If you aren't prepared with a solid response for these questions, you're still a rookie and any success you experience will be pure luck.

Now take your script and your responses and role-play them with a business partner. Practicing several times will help you relax and sound more natural when you go live. You may also want to have a set of Q-cards in front of you for quick access to easy answers. The Q-cards are a deck of cards containing responses to the most common questions and objections that come up in the invite.

Start your calls by clearing the time. "Am I catching you at a bad time or do you have a second?" If it's a bad time, tell her that you have a quick question to ask and find out when is a good time to call back. If you leave it up to her to call you back, she may forget or wait several days before getting back to you, so stay in control of the timing by getting back to her instead. If you get someone's voice mail, leave a simple message saying, "Hi, this is _____. Give me a call I have a question I want to ask you." Say no more on voice mail.

Keep your calls brief and to the point. Having too much conversation prior to inviting people to an appointment gives them the impression that the business is a minor detail so keep the main thing the main thing. Tell them up front that you only have a couple of minutes to talk. This way they know you're not calling to shoot the breeze.

Rather than setting up appointments to show the plan, new IBOs tend to make the mistake of explaining their business in casual conversation to see what kind of reaction they get. Instead of diving in, they poke at it with a stick and consequently get poor results.

Remember that the whole purpose of your invitation is just that: **it's an invitation, not information. You're not calling to explain the business; you're calling to set up an appointment.** The appointment is where they will get the information.

It's okay to answer one or two questions during your call, but don't get trapped into explaining the business. The better someone knows you, the more likely she is to press you for answers. Be prepared. In any conversation, the person asking the questions is always in control so answer a question with a question to regain control.

Here are some great questions and phrases that will help you redirect a conversation:

Statement or Question	Question for A Question
I don't know if I could do this.	Why do you say that? What exactly do you feel you couldn't do?
I prefer to shop at WalMart.	How would like to profit by the millions who don't?
I'm too busy to look at anything now.	If the money was right could you find the time?
Can you tell me more about it?	Absolutely. I'll bring an outline of the plan with me. What nights this week do you already have commitments?
Can you tell me more about it?	What do I look like an expert? However I can hook you up with the guy/gal spearheading the project. Are you available Tuesday night?
I don't think I would be interested.	What would you not be interested in?
What is it all about?	It's about making money. Does that interest you?
I think I've seen this before.	Have you seen it from me? What exactly did you see?

Let's say you have a friend who has never been to the beach before. He's never even seen a picture of it, but you know he's going to love it if you can persuade him to go with you. So you do your best to describe it to him by handing him a glass jar containing a few handfuls of sand and a few cups of salt water you got at the beach. He looks at it, shakes it up a bit, and gives you a look like you've completely lost your marbles.

Without a moment's thought, he hands the jar back to you saying, "No thanks, I don't think I'd be interested in that." Why? Because he made a judgment based solely on the contents of the jar. It was a very real piece of the beach. Nevertheless, it was just a piece. **Trying to describe this business over the phone is like handing someone a jar with sand and water. They won't get it, they won't feel it, and they won't see it.**

When making your calls to invite someone to a meeting, ask, "What nights do you already have commitments?" If he's not available on the dates of your meetings, don't even get into the script. Tell him, "Sorry. That's too bad. I'll give you a call next week and we'll see if you can make it another time." Leave him curious and he'll attend your next meeting just to find out what you're up to. If you're setting up a one-on-one appointment, go through your script first and then decide on a time to meet.

It's best to give people choices rather than asking them open-ended questions. If you ask, "Does Tuesday at 8pm work for you?" and he says "No," then you're stuck asking about Wednesday, then Thursday, and before you know it you've opened up your whole week for him. Instead, ask, "Which works better for you, Tuesday or Thursday?" This gives him more options and prevents the chase. You can also do the same with the time, "6 o'clock or 8 o'clock?"

Make sure to include the spouse when you invite people to see the plan. If your prospect hesitates to include his spouse, let him know that for the sake of time, you'd prefer to have them both present. He may be the one who makes the decisions, but he's going to talk it over with her anyway so she might as well be there so they can have an educated discussion about it.

Once you've agreed on a definite time and place to meet, it's important to confirm the appointment with him. You're double-checking his commitment to attend your meeting. To confirm your appointment, say something like, "Can I mark you down as a definite?" If he's married, you'll want to confirm that his spouse will be attending the meeting by asking, "Will your spouse be with you?" When you confirm your appointments, you'll schedule 4 meetings and show 4 plans rather than having to schedule 10 meetings to show 4 plans.

Here's a common response you'll hear when trying to confirm an appointment: "Uh, Wednesday? I think that'll work. Why don't you give me a call on Monday just to make sure." Don't agree to chase people around. Your time is valuable. Here's what you can say: "Hey Bob, I've got a lot of interviews in my calendar and I can't work that way. I either put something in my calendar and it's a done deal, or I don't. If making money isn't a priority for you right now, just let me know."

You're either going to confirm or confront. You'll either invest a little extra time and effort to confirm the appointment and lock it in ahead of time, or you're going to spend a lot of time and effort chasing people down to face an uncomfortable CONFRONTATION after the scheduled meeting dealing with why they didn't show up. Most people would rather CONFIRM than CONFRONT any day, how about you?

Invite

When Carl first got started in the business, he had an initial blast of 40 "NOs." Trying it his own way, he talked to 40 people and got nowhere. "I could barely get anyone to even look at the plan, let alone get involved. It didn't take long for my mentor to give me a pink-slip and tell me that I was fired! He said, 'Here's the new plan. You're now a talent scout for me. I'm looking for a few good people who are interested in earning $2 - $3,000 a month, part-time. Additionally, I'm willing to mentor a few of those people to earn a solid 6-figure income. Now, I want you to go talk to some people and take yourself out of the picture.'"

So he did. People would ask him questions and he would respond by saying, "Do I look like an expert to you? You need to talk to my partner. I'd be willing to put in a good word for you and set up a time when you could meet him." He started using third-party credibility by thinking of himself as a talent scout instead. Guess what? It's worked out pretty great!

Take the focus off yourself and onto the credibility of others. Whether you talk about a successful business owner, a senior associate, a good friend, author, or business trend, referring to someone or something other than yourself adds credibility to the business. And taking yourself out of the picture will lend greater credibility to your statements.

Here are some third-party approaches you can try. Let's say that you're a receptionist for a dental office and you'd like to prospect a dentist. Instead of trying to convince her about your business credibility, say something like, "I've always respected your work ethic and professionalism, would you give me your opinion on a business project I'm working on?"

Or, let's say you work in a large office and you'd like to talk to the most influential person there. You could say, "There's a bunch of people in this office that are about to become prosumers. I wanted to talk to you first because I've always respected your leadership style and I'd like to give you the opportunity to be team leader."

INVITING PHRASES

1. "Do you ever consider other ways of creating income?"

2. "If I knew a way you could _____ (achieve a specific dream / benefit of a product), would you want to hear about it?"

3. "How would you like to participate in a business project that has the potential to be bigger than WalMart?"

4. "Do you ever look at business ideas?"

5. "Did you know that there are hundreds of companies that will pay you to buy their products?"

6. "If the money was right and it fit into your schedule, would you be open to looking at a great business idea?"

7. "This could be a long shot, but a friend of mine is looking to fill a few spots on a business team and I thought of you."

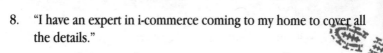

8. "I have an expert in i-commerce coming to my home to cover all the details."

9. "I can't promise you anything."

10. "A friend of mine is expanding a business and I promised him I'd keep my eyes open."

11. "I'd like to consider you as a partner on our business team."

12. "The more I've learned about this, the more I thought you may have interest or qualifications."

13. "I'd love to give you a shot at it."

CONFIRMING PHRASES

1. "How good are you at keeping your appointments?"

2. "Can I save a seat for you?"

3. "Can I mark you as a definite?"

4. "Are you just curious, or are you really looking?"

5. "I'm writing this in my calendar, are you writing it in yours?"

6. "This will be something that both you and your spouse will want to see. Will he/she be with you?"

7. "Would your spouse be involved in your decision to buy a car? Then shouldn't he/she be involved in this type of a business decision?"

8. "I won't have time to explain it twice so I'd highly recommend that your spouse be with you."

9. "We're looking to get this team assembled in the next two weeks and I'd really hate for you to miss out on this."

SHOW THE PLAN

Showing the business plan is what ignites the engine of our business. It's where we get the business in front of fresh eyes and possibility comes to life. To kick start your business as a new IBO, your support team may suggest having a home meeting where you invite several people to your home to see the business plan. In most cases, someone on your support team will be there to explain the business plan on your behalf.

Here are a few pointers to make the most of your home meetings:

Dress for success. Men, wear a coat and tie; women, wear a business dress or a skirted suit. This informs your prospects that you mean business.

Room set up. Set up chairs only as needed to avoid a room full of empty chairs. The presentation should be opposite the door to avoid interruption in case of any latecomers. Keep the room cooler than warmer so everyone is alert.

Get rid of distractions. Turn off the ringer on your home phone and ask your guests to turn off their cell phones. Have children and pets in a separate room with a sitter so that they do not interrupt the meeting.

Cater to the speaker. Save a parking spot for the speaker and assist him with any materials he may have when he arrives. How your prospects see you treat the speaker has an impact on whether they think he is worth listening to.

Keep your refreshments simple. If you serve fancy hors d'oeuvres people may think they will have to do the same to build the business. Instead, serve refreshments from your business to keep it simple. These products will also generate future volume as people are going to want to order what they sample at the meeting.

Introduction. To begin your meeting, share your excitement and your commitment to this business. Let people know that this isn't something you're just thinking about; you're focused, you're committed, and this is your ticket to achieve your dreams. When you introduce your speaker give him credibility and put your stamp of approval on him so he doesn't have to spend his time selling himself instead of the plan. Don't thank your friends for coming over - instead, during your introduction, thank your speaker for coming to your home and sharing the opportunity.

Focus on the plan. Don't run around taking care of refreshments or anything else during the meeting. Be excited, engaged, and involved in what the speaker is discussing.

Take ownership of your business as soon as possible and start showing the plan yourself. There's no need to put unnecessary pressure on yourself to get it absolutely perfect. In fact, **if your plan is any good at all the first time you show it, you've waited too long!** There's an old saying in the business that you can never show the wrong plan to the right person. In other words, it doesn't matter how bad you mess up the plan when you're showing it to someone who is teachable and motivated. So long as you convey opportunity, the right person will find their way to the information they need.

All you need to show the plan is excitement, belief, a few key points, either memorized or outlined on a brochure, and of course an audience. New IBOs typically focus on their own performance when they start to show the plan. They think of things like getting their facts and figures straight and sounding smart and successful. While we certainly do want to be informed about a business plan we're discussing, we don't want that to be the focus. The focus is what the plan can do for your prospects.

A little practice will help you grow familiar enough with the information so you can shift your focus from yourself to understanding and helping others. As mentioned earlier, confidence comes from knowing who you are, where you're going, and disciplined action. If you are undisciplined and show only one plan a month, your prospect's decision not to get involved with you is a pretty big blow to business. But if you have multiple plans lined up for the month you're thinking, "NEXT!"

To learn how to show the plan take notes while watching others explain the business at hotel and home meetings. Study an audio of someone showing the plan and start practicing on a friend, a spouse, a family member, or even a family pet. If you don't have a pet, try a stuffed animal—they smile constantly and never fall asleep!

The first time you show the plan to a key prospect on your list, ask your coach to accompany you. Together you can work as a tag-team. You introduce him as the expert. "This is John, my senior associate, he's extremely successful and I'm really excited for you that he was able to carve some time out of his busy schedule to be here." Then he tells them how successful you're going to be and why they should listen to what you're going to go over with them. You show the plan and John wraps it up. If you stumble or forget things during your plan, John is there to smooth things over.

Here are some additional things to keep in mind to
show your best plan:

• **If you're married, it's recommended that you have your spouse with you when you show the plan.** Together you have a wider range of relatability and the extra set of ears will serve to pick up on the subtleties you'd miss showing it alone. An excited couple who speaks highly of one another and works as a team adds credibility and improves their results in the business.

• **Keep your business plan informative, yet simple.** More people say "No" to this business for lack of belief than they do for lack of understanding how it all works so don't complicate it. A simple plan elicits a simple response, but **if your plan is complex, cumbersome, and detail oriented, your prospect's ability to make a decision will also be complex.** Keep it simple enough for your prospect to believe that she could easily explain it herself.

• **Stick to showing the same plan your support team shows.** If your leaders are using a yellow legal pad, use a yellow legal pad. If they're using a binder, use a binder. If they're using a booklet, use a booklet. Whatever your team is doing, duplicate it to the best of your ability to stay consistent and credible. Most teams will have several formats available for showing the plan. Use the format that works best for your prospect. If a prospect is technophobic, showing her the plan on your snazzy laptop may impress you, but it's going to leave her in the dark. If you have a prospect who is a homebody, the chances of him attending a hotel meeting for his first look at the business are slim. Whether a brochure, a binder, a whiteboard, a laptop presentation, a hotel meeting, an online meeting, or any other format, your goal is to show the plan in a way that is most relatable to each prospect while staying consistent with your support team's approach.

• **As soon as possible, read a book on personality styles.** Pick up a copy of *Positive Personality Profiles* by Dr. Robert Rohm or any other book your team recommends on the topic. Everyone is wired differently and understanding those differences will revolutionize your results and increase your tolerance of others.

• **When we promote ourselves, it's questionable at best.** When we promote others, it's credible. You want to be the messenger, not the message itself. Throughout your plan say, "Bob said this, Bob said that. Bob helped me realize this. Bob showed me how to do that." By the end of your plan, your prospect will be thinking, "I've got to meet this Bob guy!" When you introduce your prospect to Bob, he can then add to your credibility by promoting you to your prospect.

• **Maintain posture during your plan.** Posture comes from understanding the value of what you're presenting. Learn what makes your products, your business, and your team so great by talking to someone on your team who believes wholeheartedly. Understand that when you show the plan you're talking to people to see if they qualify for your business, your team, and your time; not the other way around. You need people, but you don't need any one person to succeed in the business.

Here are some examples of bad posture:
> "Please, please just do me this one favor."
> "You owe me."
> "I'm sorry for taking up your time."
> "Just get back to me whenever it's best for you."
> "I'm highly sought after and my time is worth more than yours so if you can convince me of a good reason why you deserve to work with me, I'll consider it."

Here are some examples of great Posture:

> "Let's figure out whether there's mutual interest here. If there
> isn't, we'll shake hands and wish each other all the best. If
> there is, we'll get the ball rolling."
>
> "I can't promise you anything."
>
> "Are you just curious or are you really interested in making
> money."
>
> "I'd be willing..."
>
> "We're not looking for just anyone, we're looking for a couple
> of key people."
>
> "I'd love to give you a shot at it."

Not everyone will be ripe for opportunity when you come along and present the plan to them. Sometimes you'll catch people who are skeptical and others who are discouraged, overwhelmed, or full of pretense. In any case we want to know what people are thinking so we can best help them.

People feel most comfortable talking openly with you when you take a sincere interest in understanding them first. Many of the leaders in the field refer to this as simply "making a friend." Find out about their field of work, their hobbies, and their aspirations. Ask questions about their home, their children, or the pictures on their wall. Something as simple as being a fan of the same sports team can often create instant connection with your prospects.

People also generally like people who are like them. Subtly matching a person's tone of voice, his pace, his posture, his gestures, and words makes him feel more comfortable and relaxed around you. For example, if your prospect leans back, crosses his arms, and says, "I'm just sick and tired of being a yes man. I want to call my own shots." Then leaning back and using the words "sick and tired" and "calling your own shots" somewhere in your conversation with him increases your relatability.

Tim Sanders, author of *The Likeability Factor*, offers another perspective. He asserts that "likeability," defined by the following four successive steps, is what lays the foundation for our influence with others.

1. FRIENDLINESS
Your ability to convey the message: "I like you. I'm open to you. You are Welcome."

2. RELEVANCE
"Do you relate to my daily path, my interests, or my wants and needs?" Relevance can be broken down into three elements: 1. Frequent contact 2. Mutual interest 3. Connecting with a person's basic wants and needs.

3. EMPATHY
Your ability to identify with people and invest time, attention, and emotion in their life. Are you available to feel and experience what they experience?

4. REAL
It's all about "keeping it real." Someone who finds you unreal will no longer believe you are sincerely friendly, they will feel any relevance you had was concocted, and they will conclude that your empathy was only sympathy with a twist. In other words, you don't really identify with your feelings - you're just a good actor.

How's your "Likeability Factor"? Are you merely looking to register people so they'll do some volume in your business, or are you looking to partner in business with them, to get to know them, and help them improve their life? Drop a little sunlight in their life; believe in what they can achieve and experience the excitement of their dreams and goals with them. That alone brings something to the table that most people aren't getting anywhere else.

Before getting into the details of the plan, it's important to understand what your prospect would like to achieve. His understanding of how the business works is secondary to what he wants out of it, not because you're trying to deceive him and hide information from him, but because you can't help him until you know what he wants.

Let's say he wants to make an additional couple hundred dollars a month to pay down some bills. But you neglect to gather that information so you show him a plan to replace his entire income, buy a motor home, and travel around the world while helping thousands of people gain their financial independence. After hearing your plan, he comes to the conclusion that he isn't interested and consequently misses out on a great opportunity to make a few extra bucks. How have you helped him?

It's also important for a prospect to understand what he's going to get out of it before seeing the work involved so he can reasonably decide whether it's worth it or not. Every price is relative to its prize. No one wants to work overtime, but many do for the extra money. No one wants to pay interest, but many do to extend payment. Likewise, people don't build the business just to build a business, they build it for what they can gain in return.

Some people you show the plan to will already know precisely what they want – others will need some help figuring it out. Don't tell people what they need by saying, "Gees, you're broke, your job stinks, and your life is miserable. Think of how great it will be when…" Most everyone is doing the best they can with what they know - just like you and I did before we saw the plan - so don't criticize. Instead, ask them questions and let them tell you.

In his book, *Questions are the Answer*, Allan Pease writes that when you talk to people about this business, they expect that you are going to try and convince them to make a commitment. They are waiting for you to start selling and naturally, no one wants to be sold no matter how well they may know you. So right from the start, you are most likely talking to someone who has taken a defensive stance towards what you are about to say, simply because it is your idea, not theirs.

Lead people to their own conclusions by asking a series of questions and they will automatically agree with it and believe it to be true—because *they* said it. It is *their* idea, not yours; and people rarely argue with themselves.

Pease suggests the following approach to find a person's reason: he states that research has shown that most people's **Primary Motivating Factors** for getting involved in this business are one of the following:

> Extra income
> Financial freedom
> Have own business
> More spare time
> Personal development
> Helping others
> Meeting new people
> Retirement
> Leave a legacy

Present your prospects with this list and ask them these three questions: "Which is most important to you?" "Why is that one most important to you?" and "What would be the consequences of never achieving it?" Listen carefully to each of their answers. If you sense that they are uncomfortable, tell them which one you picked and why. Don't be surface about your reasons for building the business. Speak from your heart and let others feel the full impact of who you are. In today's busy world where people are constantly bombarded by the urgent, a nice pleasant conversation about an interesting business plan just isn't going to cut it. You need to have impact somehow in the brief amount of time you have with them.

Here's an example of asking questions to uncover a person's reason:

IBO: "So tell me Bob, you have a great job, a comfortable lifestyle, and a wonderful family life. Why would you have any interest in taking a look at a business idea?"

Bob: "I'd like to make more money."

IBO: "More money…?"

Bob: "It seems like no matter how hard I work I'm just not getting any further ahead."

IBO: "What does getting further ahead look like to you?"

Bob: "Well, we'd really like to buy a house. This condo is just too small for us and it's not much of a home if you know what I mean."

IBO: "How do you mean?"

Bob: "It's just that there's not enough room for any of us to relax and enjoy each other. The kids want to run around, my wife wants to have people over and entertain, I want to work on my projects every now and then, but we're all having to compromise because we can't afford the space. It's really getting to be a strain on our family.

IBO: "A strain on your family?"

Bob: "Yeah, there's just a lot of tension between us and it's causing us to argue more and more."

IBO: "I'm sorry to hear that. What kind of projects do you like to work on Bob?"

Bob: "My father was a mechanic and I guess his passion for older cars rubbed off on me. I'd love nothing more than to find some old clunker and fix it up into a real beauty, but I don't have the money or the space to do those kinds of things right now."

IBO: "Bob, are all of those things important to you? Less tension in the home, your wife being able to entertain, your kids having room to play, your passion for cars, and not having to compromise what you truly want?"

Bob: "You bet."

IBO: "Why?"

Bob: "Because I know my wife and kids deserve more than this crummy little condo. My kids take off to their friends' houses instead of inviting their friends here. And when I see the way my wife talks about the homes she sees it really gets to me. I can't stand not being able to give her what she wants, I just don't know what else I can do."

IBO: "It sounds like getting into the right house could really change a lot of things for you and your family. I hope you don't mind that I'm asking you these questions because they're important. I want to make sure I understand what you're trying to achieve. The more I understand where you're coming from, the more I'll be able to help you accomplish those things."

Bob: "Sure."

IBO: "Bob, what if you kept doing what you're doing now and never could get ahead and buy a home? What would that mean for you and your family?"

Bob: "I can't imagine working like this forever and staying where we are. I guess that would mean I'd never be able to give them what they really deserve. I know a house isn't everything, but our family is. And we're just not happy being limited the way we are here. We're frustrated because we're not able to do what we really enjoy and I don't want my wife and kids to have to live like that anymore."

IBO: "Is it safe to say then that finding a way to buy the right house for your family is a priority for you right now?"

Bob: "Absolutely."

IBO: "Bob, I'm glad to hear that because I'm looking to work with a few people who are serious about achieving their dreams and goals. I can't promise you anything, but the business plan I'm about to show you may be the opportunity you've been looking for. If you're not opposed to putting some focused effort into a worthwhile project, I believe that you and your family will live in that home. And when you accomplish that, I'll feel like a success. On a personal level, I really like you and your family and think you'd be a great partner to work with. What do you think? Can you imagine what it's going to be like when your wife walks up to her new home for the very first time? What do you think she's going to be feeling when she turns the key and opens that door?"

Do you think Bob's excited about working with this IBO? What would this IBO have missed if he had started showing the plan after Bob said, "I want to make more money"? Did Bob "experience" his dream emotionally? And do you think he sees the business opportunity as something that's going to help him change his future, rather than just some distant and inconsequential presentation?

The IBO could have further questioned Bob to find out the approximate cost of the home, what the monthly payment on a mortgage would be, etc. in order to quantify the goal and focus his plan with that end in mind. But the most important thing the IBO did do is to uncover Bob's primary reason. Now, when Bob sees the plan, he's not only going to see a business, he's going to see a solution.

The art of questioning is one of the most invaluable skills you will learn to increase your persuasiveness. The more questions you ask aimed at finding a need or uncovering discontent, the more interest people will have and the more persuasive you become. Great questions will lead people to begin visualizing and imagining what their life will be like with and without their dream. And when people really see and believe in the possibilities of a greater future through their involvement in the business, they will act on it.

Notice in the example how the IBO took time to listen and ask more questions about Bob's responses before piping in with his own response? How well do you listen when people talk? Are you thinking about what people are saying or are you busy preparing in your mind what you're going to say next? There's a difference between hearing and listening. If you aren't hearing-impaired, hearing happens involuntarily. Listening, however, is something you consciously choose to do. It's where you concentrate on understanding the meaning behind a person's words.

Most of us hear only a portion of what someone is saying before we try to fit it into our own categories. As a result, we often misunderstand people and our responses are off target. To fine-tune your listening skills, practice waiting until a person is completely finished talking and then pause before you start talking. You can also improve your level of listening by repeating back to people what you heard them say. "So what you're saying is…" or "Let me make sure I understand you correctly … is that right?" Then give them a chance to correct you or add to their original statement.

Always incorporate a sense of urgency when you show the plan. What do people have to lose if they don't get involved now? Listen to your leaders as they show the plan and note how they create urgency. Do they discuss favorable trends and timing? Do they talk about a team that is exploding right now? Is there a special event coming up? Learn from your leaders and incorporate these aspects into your business plan. Additionally, if you have people on your list who your prospect also knows, let him know that those potential IBOs could be in his business if he were to get started first.

After showing your prospects the plan, it's time to determine their level of interest. Some IBOs take the time to prospect, invite, and show the plan to people, and then walk out the door without ever asking about their interest level! These IBOs expect that people are going to ask them to get registered in the business, buy some training materials, and schedule their first home meeting. Dream on.

We need to lead by asking, "So where do you see yourself with this business?" or "What did you like best about what we've discussed?" One common approach is to tell people that most everyone who sees this business plan finds themselves in one of three categories:

1. This looks great. I may have a couple of questions, but **I'm ready to start making money right away.**
2. I'm definitely interested, but **I'd like to get some more information** and meet the team before I start making money.
3. I'm not interested in making money, but **I would be interested in trying some exclusive products** and enjoying the convenience of home delivery.

Set the right expectancy by highlighting #1. If you say, "Whether you're a 1, or a 2, we're telling everyone to get registered right away so you can reserve your spot on the team. We'll set you up with some information to take home with you, schedule a time to get back together to answer any questions you may have, and help you get started before you miss out on any of the growth we've been experiencing. If you're a 3, we'll get you registered as a customer tonight and send you home with some products you can try. What's the result in this scenario? Everyone is expected to register as either an IBO or a customer NOW.

Often times we run into questions and objections about the business at the close of the plan, which we'll cover in the next chapter. For now, let's assume that your prospects say that they are interested in getting started and getting more information. ALWAYS, always have first night materials available to leave with your prospects when you show the plan. In addition to first night materials, make sure to promote your team's upcoming events like hotel opens and training events where they can meet the team, see the bigger picture, and begin learning about the business. Have tickets on hand so they can purchase them and make their commitment to attend right away.

Prospects in this business are notorious for flip-flopping in their commitments like a fish out of water until they either listen to some audios, see tangible results, and/or attend a major event so have materials and tickets on hand and learn to promote them well.

One diamond in the business kept a notebook and every time he listened to a CD, he would write down the name of the CD, who the speaker was, and the gist of what that CD talked about. He would write things like, "Negative spouse" or "Didn't have time" so that he would know exactly which CD to hand people. He created a personal library of materials to make sure he'd be prepared to do business out of the trunk of his car.

Diamond Stories

Only send your materials home with people who you have a follow through meeting booked with or you will lose them. Make your prospect aware of the value of your materials by saying, "I'll need to get these materials back in a couple of days. How soon do you think you'll be able to get through them?" If she replies, "Well, I don't want to keep them if you need them. I'll just borrow them from you another time." Then that's an indication that learning more about the business is not a priority for her at this time.

Don't insist and say, "Well here, take them and I'll get them from you in a couple of days." You might as well tell her you're desperate for anyone to get in your business and you're hoping she's it. If she won't book a follow through, she won't commit to attending an event, and she isn't interested in learning more, it's game over. Ask for a referral or check back with her in a few months because you won't be able to work with someone like that.

Save your materials for people who value them who are interested in learning more. Have every prospect that you show the plan to fill out some sort of information card so you have their name, address, home phone, cell phone, and e-mail address. Ask them when is the best time to reach them and at which phone number. And remember to always, always, **ALWAYS book a meeting from a meeting.** Just like taking an international trip with multiple layovers, when you miss one connection, the whole thing falls apart. Excitement dwindles, life happens, priorities shift, and your prospect will fall through the cracks. The business may be important to them, but it's competing with what's urgent in their life, so make it a priority and set up your next meeting with them before you leave.

It's a good idea to invite your prospect to a hotel meeting, but you also want to have a separate time scheduled with them incase they don't show up. When you do invite people to a hotel meeting offer to pick them up at their home. Being in the car together will give you some valuable talk time and will also prevent them from changing their mind about attending the meeting after a long day at work.

Once your prospects get registered in the business you must lead them through the process of getting started. Just because someone signs a registration form and says he wants to build the business doesn't mean it's time for you to go home, sit back on the couch, and count your bankroll. You've only just begun the process and now is when the real work in your business begins. Help him make a names list, role-play, make phone calls, show plans, go over products and Ditto Scheduled Orders™.

Sound like real work? Absolutely. But it is work that will continue to pay you for life. Years later as you're living your dreams, when the work you invested is but a distant memory, you'll still be getting checks in the mail rewarding you for the disciplined actions you took today. Is it worth it? That's for you to decide.

FOLLOW THROUGH

Follow through is the process that begins after your prospect sees
the business plan. There are many situations you will deal with
in the follow through so the key is to be prepared and to remain
flexible. 10% of the people you show the plan to will say, "Yes" no
matter what you say or do. Another 10% will say, "No" regardless of
who shows them the plan. The remaining 80% will sway either way
depending on what you do.

At your follow through meeting you'll want to revisit their dream,
determine their level of interest, answer any questions or objections
they may have, build their belief, and get them started in the process
of building their business. The ideal result of the follow through
process is to have a prospect who:

- has registered in the business as an IBO
- has set some goals
- has a written names list
- has set up a Ditto Scheduled Order™ that processes on the
  first of every month (DOT1).
- is engaged in your team's training system (attending events,
  listening, reading, etc.)
- has meetings (for people on his list to see the plan)
  scheduled with confirmed attendees.

Some prospects will fly through this list while others will need
coaxing every step of the way. Be prepared to meet people at their
needs. Your initial follow through meeting should happen within
24 to 48 hours after you show your prospect the plan. That is your
window of opportunity when excitement levels are at their peak and
possibility is still fresh in her mind. It's always best to meet face to
face, but if that's impossible connect with her by phone.

REVISIT THEIR DREAM

At your meeting be awake, alert, and excited because you're helping someone start a business. You're bringing an atmosphere that's fun, hopeful, and full of possibility with you. Start by taking a few minutes to rekindle the friendship and the dream. You can say something like, "You know that boat you were talking about the other night? Well, I've decided that I'm going to have to help you get it so I can borrow it."

We don't use people to build our business; we use our business to build people. And you can't build people or help them move forward in this business without understanding what's important to them. If you have to write down notes after each plan you show to remember what's important to each person - dreams and goals, names of family members, etc. - then do it.

Everything in this business hinges on relationships so work on being someone people enjoy being around. People want to spend time with those who make them feel good about themselves. Talk to them about their unique qualities and how you see those qualities contributing to their business. Be specific in your praise and begin painting the picture of their success for them.

DETERMINE THEIR LEVEL OF INTEREST

Once you reconnect with people and bring their dream back to the forefront, it's time to determine their level of interest. Questions like, "Where would you like to see yourself with this?" or "What did you like best about the materials I left you?" or "What do you say we go ahead and secure your position on the team?" will help you determine their readiness to get started in the business.

Some people will be ready to get started right away, some will have questions and/or objections, some will want to be members and/or clients, and some won't want to be involved at all. As a professional in the field, you want to handle your prospect's decisions objectively. It's natural to feel excited, happy, disappointed, or angry when prospects state their level of interest - especially if you've already formed your own expectations for them. But when our emotions go up, our intelligence goes down so expect the best and recognize the possibility of anything less.

If someone turns out to be a "No," ask for a referral by saying, "Bob, I can see that you're not interested in getting involved at this time and that's fine. We're looking to fill a few key spots on the team in the next couple of weeks. Who do you know that might be a good candidate and a match for what we're looking for?"

When you call a referral you can say, "This is _____, we haven't met yet, but we have a mutual friend through Bob. I'm working on a business project and he thought you might have interest and qualifications in what I'm looking for. I can't promise you anything, but let me ask you, are you open to taking a look at a business idea?" A referral is a stronger lead than a person you meet without any previous relationship so take the time to ask for them.

People who say "No" to the business are prime candidates to become customers. Let them try some samples and refer them to your personalized web site. Talk to them about the benefits of our exclusive products, the convenience of home delivery, and our money back guarantee. Let them know you'd love to earn as much of their business as they think you deserve.

ANSWER QUESTIONS AND OVERCOME OBJECTIONS

When you're faced with prospects who have questions or objections, listen to what they have to say. Unfortunately, not all prospects are as transparent as we'd like them to be so our questioning, listening, and persuading skills will be especially valuable here. When faced with objections, we don't want to discount our prospect's concerns, prove him wrong, beg him, or shrink away with our tail between our legs. What we want is to understand where he's coming from so we can get to the heart of the matter and help him.

You will find that there are about half a dozen objections that people will give you. They don't have time, they can't afford it, they don't like to sell, etc. Learn and practice your responses. Good answers to some of the more common questions and objections are outlined for you in the last section of this book. Read through them as often as necessary and think about how you'll respond when you get those objections.

The typical prospect will have somewhere between two to three objections before making a final decision. Understand that questions and objections don't necessarily indicate lack of interest. In fact, people who have no interest usually don't ask anything at all. It's the ones who are thinking who ask questions. It means they're mulling it over.

Questions and objections are often just a knee-jerk reaction people have to avoid making a decision they are unsure of. It's also common for people to bring up a few surface objections before letting you in on their main concern so listen carefully and avoid any lengthy responses until you know it's a major. In fact, if you can get to the main issue and resolve it, many of the other surface concerns will often resolve themselves.

For example: if someone says, "I don't know enough people to make this work." Your natural instinct may be to tackle that issue immediately. But if instead you ask, "Aside from knowing enough people is there anything else keeping you from getting involved?" You can then uncover all her concerns and tackle the most important one first. Once you feel that she's brought up all of her concerns confirm it by asking, "If we can work through these concerns is there anything else that would prevent you from accomplishing_____ (her dream/goal)?"

Instead of answering every question, point people to the audios for answers. Time and again the leaders in this business have stated that it was hearing the heart-gripping story of someone who made it in the business that was the deciding factor for them.

Underneath all the smoke and mirrors, most everyone will have one primary motivating factor compelling them to get involved in the business. They will also have one primary objection that, left unaddressed, will sway them from doing so. The greater your ability to uncover these two factors, overcome the objection (yourself or by audio), and amplify the reason, the greater your success will be in getting people involved.

Make a point to validate your prospect's concern and find out if she is looking for a solution. "I understand that you don't think you know enough people. In fact, I don't even know if you know enough people to make this work. But I do know that we have a program that can help you - if you really want to focus on the reward of what this business can do for you."

So often people reply, "You've been on the planet for 30 years! You do know enough people. What about your teacher, your doctor, your parents…" And the result is an argument where your prospect is forced to defend her original statement. You may win the battle, but you'll lose the war. Don't argue and discount what people say – agree with them. Because they either really believe their objection or they're just looking for some reassurance.

Agree with people and then refocus them in the direction of their prize. "You're right, you don't have time. You're working two jobs trying to make ends meet and you barely have any time with your family as it is, let alone a business project. I know it's not easy, but what if? What if you were to scrounge up just a few hours a week to put into a business of your own, where in the next 90 days you were able to replace the income from your second job, and in a few months, both jobs? What would it be worth to walk away from those jobs and never have to work for another man or woman for the rest of your life? Would it be worth prioritizing your time temporarily to achieve that?"

As you listen to your prospect, the question you're looking to answer is, "Is this person looking to find a solution or are they just looking for an excuse?" You can always help the person who has a valid concern, who truly wants to overcome the obstacles to achieve their dream. But when someone is just looking for an excuse, nothing you say or do will matter because they're not interested in being helped.

For example, IBOs often hear from friends, "When you make your first million, I'll give it a try." What your friend is saying is that he doesn't believe you're going to stick it out. This friend is not as ready as you are to take initiative, nor is he a good candidate for your business team. Instead of trying to convince him otherwise, move on.

The key to weeding out the excuses is to gain clarity. Don't settle for anything vague; get specific answers instead. One of the most common responses we hear from prospects is "Let me think about it and I'll call you." Most IBOs wait until the drive home to start wondering *What are they going to think about? When are they going to call?* Your steering wheel can't answer those questions, but your prospects can so ask them.

When someone says he'll think about it say, "What is it you need to think about? If you have questions and concerns, let's bring them to the table so we can discuss them while I'm here." If he says he'd rather think about it on his own, ask him what he's going to think about and what his time frame is. If hc's going to call you, find out when you can expect his call and set up a specific date that you will call by if you don't hear from him.

If he becomes uncomfortable with your questions, let him know that it's important for you to know what he's thinking so you know how best to follow through with him. There's nothing unreasonable about asking these questions so long as you keep a smile on your face and maintain a cool demeanor. If he's clearly skirting every issue with you, he's most likely looking for an excuse. Give him a way out and be clear that you're not interested in playing games. Say, "Bob, if you need to think about things, I'm okay with that. This is important and I want you to make a quality decision. But if you're just looking for an excuse, then I probably need to know that."

When you make it easy for people to say "No" they will. When you make it difficult for people to say "No" they'll tell you "Maybe" to avoid the confrontation and then they'll stop returning your calls because they really mean "No." Why waste your time chasing a "No" when you could be talking to a "Yes" instead?

The greatest clues to whether your prospects are sincere about their interest in the business are found not in what they say, but in what they do. Have they listened to the audios you left them? Did they crack the book? Did they attend the meeting? Actions are the telltale signs of a person's priorities.

When handling objections, don't always jump to explanation. Try asking questions instead to find your way to a solution. For example, if someone says, "I can get these products cheaper at Costco®." you could ask, "Do you always buy the very cheapest products? Have you ever bought anything that wasn't the lowest price? Why?" Or, "Is there anything we have that you can't get at Costco®?" Or, "Is there any reason you can think of that would make you consider buying products through your own business?"

Sometimes we come across people who are stuck in a state of limbo. They seem to want to get involved, but for one reason or another, they just can't seem to make that final decision. To help them over the hump and to assure them that they are making the right decision, try mapping out the best, worst, and realistic case scenario for them. Here's how:

You: "Bob, I can see you're having trouble making a decision. Let me give you the three possible scenarios of what can happen from here. Let's say your team grew to 100 people in a few months and 1,000 in one year, would you be excited?"

Bob: "Of course."

You: "Of course, and that would be a best case scenario. Now, let's say you join our team and for $_____ you get some great training, some great products, and have access to one of the largest shopping sites on the web. But you decide to do absolutely nothing with the business. You make a rebate on all of your purchases, enjoy the convenience of home delivery, and benefit from the tax advantages. Bob, if this is what happened, could you live with that?"

Bob: "Sure."

You: "Great, let's talk about the realistic case scenario. You start tonight, and in a few weeks we've added a few people to your team, and in a few months you have over 25 people on your team. By the end of one year, you have over 100 people in your organization and you're making anywhere from $500 to $2,000 a month. You've added some financial security and more time with your family. Bob, if that were about to happen to you, would that change your lifestyle for the better?"

Bob: "Yes it would."

You: "Then let me ask you this Bob, are you willing to make a decision and risk the worst case scenario in order to get to the realistic case scenario, and possibly the best case scenario?"

Bob: "Yes, I think I am."

You: "In that case, here's what I recommend..."

Mapping out the possibilities for Bob eliminates his fear of making a wrong decision and you're also building trust by openly discussing the worst case scenario with him.

Many of the leaders in the business recommend using the "feel, felt, found" method to overcome objections. "I know how you feel, I felt the same way, here's what I found..." Whether you use these exact words or not this method has impact because you're sharing your own personal experience. These types of stories show that you understand and they have influence on people because they're personal.

For example if you were inviting someone to a hotel meeting you could say, "Bob, it'd be great for you to go to this next meeting. It's at this hotel, on this date, at this time. You'll learn a lot by seeing the business plan again and meeting the team." In this example you've informed Bob.

Now compare that to: "Bob, I remember sitting here just like you looking at this idea for the first time wondering, 'Could this business really work for me?' It wasn't until I went to a hotel meeting where I met all kinds of people who were building this business that it really started to make sense for me. I saw a young man show the business plan that night and he talked about how he had earned his freedom as a result of this idea. He answered a lot of my questions and made this business real to me. The more I saw, the more I realized that I could do this. I'm so grateful today that I took a few hours out of my life to see if this idea could work for me." Feel the difference? If you find the same objections coming up, over and over, consider incorporating them into your plan. In other words, handle the objection during your plan before your prospect has a chance to bring it up himself.

One diamond who got sick of hearing that the reason people didn't want to get involved was because they didn't like to shop online decided to address the objection in his plan. As he talked about the mega-trend of online shopping, he'd say, "Look, it's not a matter of whether you like to shop on line, it's whether you are willing to shop online. You don't have to be a woman to own a woman's clothing store and you don't have to like donuts to own and profit from a donut shop. It's not a matter of what you personally like, it's about understanding the trends in the marketplace and whether you're smart about making money. People are going to shop online whether you like to or not. And whether you get involved or not, this mega-trend will happen. So the question is: Are you going to make money with it?"

When leading your prospects to make their decision, rather than pressuring them to make an all out "I'm going to do this!" decision, try easing them into taking baby steps. In his classic book of positive persuasion skills titled *Winning Without Intimidation*, author, Bob Burg, suggests planting questions in the affirmative. He gives the following example:

> Let's say you're going to ask someone out on a dinner date. Which of these three ways do you think would elicit the most positive response?

#1. "You wouldn't want to go out to dinner with me, would you?"
#2. "Would you like to go out to dinner with me?"
#3. "If we were to go to dinner, where would you most like to go?"

Number three is the only question that is set up so that within the answer is the "Yes" response. If the person you are asking responds by saying, "Oh, I'd like to go to the Lobster House Restaurant," they have actually said, "Yes, I'd like to go out with you … to the Lobster House Restaurant."

Asking these types of questions gets people picturing their involvement and takes the pressure off of having to make a difficult decision. Instead of having to say, "Yes, I'll do it!" They're able to say, "If I did do it, I would…"

Here are some other examples of planting the affirmative:
"Let's say you did get involved, would your schedule permit you to attend our next team meeting?"
"Let's say you talk it over with your spouse and she gets excited, how soon would you want to meet the team?"
"If you knew for a fact that the first person you called was going to get involved in business with you, who would you call first?"
"If you did decide to build the business, what would be your number one reason for doing so?"

People rarely say things like, "I'm ready!" or "Sign me up!" when they're ready to get involved. Instead, they typically say things like, "I guess there's nothing to lose." Or they'll ask involvement questions like, "So what would we be doing?" or "When did you say that next meeting was?" When you hear these types of comments, take the lead and say, "Here's what I recommend: Let's go ahead and take care of the registration, you can come out to the meeting on Tuesday and meet the team, and then before we leave tonight we'll pencil in a time to go over our game plan."

BUILD THEIR BELIEF

Throughout the follow through process you want to build your prospect's belief. "I think we're going to make a lot of money together." "I think we're going to have a lot of fun building the business together." Remember to talk in terms of what's important to her. "I think… I think… I think…" While her belief is fragile, give her the reassurance she needs by affirming her decision and verbalizing your belief in her."

Building belief doesn't end with the initial follow through meeting. You don't stop loving your spouse and courting him/her after the wedding unless you want a stale marriage. And you don't stop encouraging people on your team unless you want a small business. We all need to hear that we have what it takes and that it's worth it - over and over again - because our belief is being tested over and over again.

A key to building strong belief within your team can be found in the joke, "How do you know when an entrepreneur is selling? His lips are moving!" Never stop selling, or what we call promoting and edifying, in every area of your business. Promote your support team, the audio you listened to or the book you read, the training events, the voicemail you heard, the products, the great experience you had dealing with customer service, the favorable economic trends, the success people are having, the improvements they're making – promote everything; all of the time.

START THE PROCESS

So far we've discussed the process of making a names list, inviting, showing the plan, and following through. You've performed these steps yourself. Now it's time to walk your new IBOs through these same steps.

Just like the plan, we want to keep things simple. If there's any confusion or hesitation on your part, doubt will set in. And when there's doubt all activity ceases, so keep it basic. All we are trying to teach people to do is learn a process of five simple steps (names list, invite, show the plan, follow through, repeat the process) that, when repeated enough times, they can turn around and teach someone else how to do the same. It's that simple.

When getting your prospects started, imagine that they only have 30 days left to live. In other words, make something happen before grass starts growing under their feet. People need to see results quickly before their belief is affected so set the expectation for action upfront.

Whether it's making a names list, setting up a Ditto Scheduled Order™, or anything else that needs to happen in order for them to succeed, be upfront about it. If people are hesitant about taking action, let them know that their business will not grow without people and product. Say, "I'd love to tell you to wait until you're completely comfortable with the business before you order product and talk to people, but let's be honest here - if in a couple of month's time, you don't see results in your business, you're going to quit and say that the business doesn't work. And I'm not interested in setting people up to fail - it's my responsibility to help you win. If you're not ready to get started right now that's okay. I'd be happy to take care of you as a customer. But if you are ready, let's do this right and start putting some money in your pocket."

Why waste time registering someone who is going to do zero volume or who is unwilling to make a names list? Every time you and your team see that name pop up on the Line of Sponsorship with a big fat zero next to it, it's going to work against you. Don't try to persuade your prospects by making it seem easier for them. Instead, set greater expectations for joining your team. There is nothing more motivating to a new IBO than to see the business actually work, and that will happen when you get people started right. Her first bonus check, her first new IBO, her first time crossing stage; these are what make it easier for IBOs to build their business.

Zero's

LEADERSHIP & DUPLICATION

The founding philosophy of any business in our industry is one word: duplication. Duplication is the goal, duplication is the magic, and duplication is what will allow you to live the life of your dreams.

If the only way you learn how to make your business grow is through your efforts alone, then the only thing you have is a glorified job because it won't work without you. Growing your business beyond the extent of your own physical effort requires duplication. And when it's done right, duplication equals paid freedom: getting paid continuously while having the freedom to live the lifestyle of your dreams.

Imagine having 10, 100, 1,000, or 10,000 people in your business duplicating the very same effort you're putting forth in your business today. If that's music to your ears you're on the right track. If not, it's time to start working on the most essential element of duplication: YOU.

The truth is, **whether you decide to lead or not, the people on your team are going to look to you for leadership.** And right or wrong, the precedent you set will be followed. What you do affects everyone around you and the moment we stop making excuses and start taking that responsibility seriously, we begin initiating ourselves into the ranks of leadership.

If you want a great team, be great. It's that simple. Lukewarm, mildly interested, mousy IBOs don't inspire teams to action; commitment does. Ghandi, Mother Theresa, and Martin Luther King didn't inspire people because of what they believed; they were an inspiration to millions because despite their obstacles they committed their lives to their cause.

Lead

68

Looking at the leaders in our business, here's what you'll find they're committed to:

Association. 80% of success is just showing up. Your team cannot count on you without your predictable presence in the business. Make one decision to attend everything your leadership attends and stick to it. If your leaders think it's worth their time to be there, it's worth yours. Get the schedule, put it in your calendar, budget for the cost, and make whatever arrangements are necessary in advance.

Associating with your leaders is also the fastest way for you to succeed. Studying people who have already paid the price to learn the things you need to learn, and doing what they do, saves you the time and effort of having to learn it all yourself. The obvious opportunities to learn from your leaders are: training events, hotel meetings, leaderships, etc. Some not so obvious opportunities are: before and after events and meetings and after hours at the coffee shop. These are the times when you can tune in to valuable discussions that may teach you more than what you hear from stage.

Profitability. Guess what? You are in a word-of-mouth, sales and marketing business where your profitability depends on you. There are no advertisements – you're it! Be a walking, talking advertisement for the products and services you market. To establish predictable profitability within your team, commit to Dot1 (Ditto on the first). Duplicating a simple team standard of Dot1 – setting up a Ditto Scheduled Order™ to process on the 1st of every month increases the average PV per team member by the end of each month while also affording teams a full month's time to strategize towards their goals.

If you're not teaching your team about product loyalty and profitability, you're setting them up to fail. There is no profitability without product volume in this business and if you're not setting that expectation upfront, you're missing the boat on profitability. We're not talking about stockpiling widgets; we're talking hot, cutting-edge products like XS™ drinks, Gensona™ genetic testing kits, and NAO™ cosmetics. Anybody could eat their way to personal PV with the "incredible edibles" we have available today.

Positive promotion. Talk a little louder and prouder about what you've got your hands on. Focus your promotion on what makes your business grow and profit: meetings and training events, team goals, unity, fun, excitement, profitability, and making a difference. Promote the good in others and promote the products and services you love. Avoid gossip and trash talk. If you're not part of the problem or part of the solution, don't talk about it. Don't waste your words perpetuating problems, focus on finding solutions and creating a positive buzz within your team.

Personal growth. Many of us aren't accustomed to stretching and growing when we start our business. Perhaps we've spent years in a position where we simply repeated the same things over and over again without ever being challenged to move outside of our comfort zone. When we begin building this business, we find that our old comfortable patterns don't apply so well. We realize that if we are to succeed we'll need to do things we've never done before.

There is no better arena for growth than the personal and professional development system put in place by your leadership. It's far more comforting to grow together with a team then it is to have to grow individually. And it's much easier to grow into leadership when there are multiple examples to follow. In life we get beat up a bit by financial situations, family situations, and other things that sap our belief and energy. The system serves as a constant encouragement and positive influence to keep us keeping on.

Find people in your support team who can mentor you to greater levels of success. Unlike your friends, a mentor will stretch you out of your comfort zone to help you become all that you can be. A friend will agree with you and validate your excuses while a mentor will challenge and encourage you to rise above the excuses. No matter how great a mentor is he can only be as effective as you are willing.

When Rick first started building his business, like many of us, he thought his circumstances were too big to overcome. "I used to take my big ugly problems to my mentor and say, 'Look at this big ugly thing. It's ugly!' I thought he'd say, 'Yeah, let's let it kill us both!' But he didn't. Instead, he taught me about attitude. He'd say, 'You know, the average person would get hung up on that. What are *you* going to do?' Other times he'd ask me, 'Do you want a raise?' And I'd answer, 'Of course I want a raise!' He'd say, 'Then you figure out a way to deal with it.' That used to tick me off so bad, but he was teaching me how to be a problem solver, not a problem enhancer."

Think long-term. In business there are ups and downs. Some days you'll feel like the whole world is against you and other days everything will click and turn in your favor. A leader feels the same emotions we do when we're in the thick of a down turn. But rather than getting wrapped up in every moment, rushing to judgment about their business with every turn of events, a leader concentrates on the big picture. Instead of basing their success on the outcome of any one meeting, they evaluate their overall progress after showing a series of meetings. Rather than "trying it out" for a month, they commit to giving it their honest effort for a year. Napoleon said that the chief characteristic of an effective soldier is not courage, but endurance. Likewise, the chief characteristic of an IBO is consistency - the capacity to keep going, keep moving in the direction of his goals, despite the circumstances that surround him.

Work towards a goal. If you don't have a goal, you're going to hit it with amazing accuracy. Sit down with someone on your support team and talk to him about what you want to accomplish. Find out what kind of work is involved. How many plans will you have to show? What will you have to do to achieve your goal? If you're just getting started, you can set a date to show your first plan or to set up a Dot1. Find out what type of recognition your support team has at your team events and set a goal to cross the stage at your next event.

Set goals around the vital signs of your business: achievement level on the bonus chart, individual and group product volume, number of new IBOs, number of IBOs on Ditto, number of IBOs attending monthly training events, number of IBOs subscribed to the continuing education program, number of plans being shown in the group, etc. Additionally, tying your goals to the achievement of key members in your team will help you develop leadership.

When you don't hit a goal, reset it. Don't quit setting goals just because you didn't hit it – that's about as ridiculous as throwing your car away because you didn't get home on time. The goal itself isn't what is significant – it's progress that matters. Maybe you set it too high or you didn't understand the work involved. Learn from it and move on. When you hit a goal, set the marker a little bit higher the following month to continually stretch yourself.

A goal left unachieved for too long will no longer motivate, but de-motivate you. Change it up, break it up, or focus on a different angle - just keep trying and re-set new goals. Reward yourself proportionately for the goals that you do achieve to help reinforce the process. You wouldn't buy yourself a Lamborghini for showing 15 plans in one month, but you would treat yourself to an inexpensive lunch or download that new album you want for your iPod.

If you aren't achieving goals, it may be that you have no one to answer to. Maybe you've gone a month, six months, or even a year without making any progress because no one has called you on it. It's possible that no one ever will unless you ask someone to hold you accountable for what you know you are capable of accomplishing. Set up a time to meet with someone on your support team and ask for help. Talk about what you'd like in an accountability partner and be open to suggestion.

The role of an accountability partner is to make it uncomfortable for you not to hold up your end of the bargain. "Here's what you said you were going to do, here's why you said that was important to you, here's what you did, what's up? I know what you've got inside of you and this isn't it." Hitting your goals and communicating with your accountability partner is your responsibility. Don't expect them to call you and check up on you every day; you call.

Take responsibility. You are responsible for your business, your team, your growth, your relationships, your finances, and your circumstances. The buck stops with you. Some of us have signed the registration form giving us the right to become business owners, but we're still acting like employees. We wait for our support team to tell us to go to the next event, to try the new product, to set a goal, and to make phone calls. How do you know when you have employee mentality? You make excuses for why you can't build *your* business!

Want a raise? Go earn it. Want more excitement at the meetings? Create it. Want better leadership? Become it. It's your business. Support in this business is not something you have a right to; it's something you're blessed with. Be grateful for what you do have and take responsibility for creating the change you desire.

Lead

When Rick and Valerie pulled up in front of their IBOs house to show the plan and saw there were no cars there, they felt relieved. Instead of having to show the plan to someone new, they'd have an easy night developing relationships with their IBOs. Then after a while Rick started thinking, "You know what? I can't take the easy way out my whole life. Somewhere along the line, we've got to get serious and we've got to build our business." So Rick and Valerie started making everything count. They started getting focused on results rather than just taking the journey and that's when things started to happen.

In our business there is a leadership continuum that looks something like this:

Prospect ➡ Pro-sumer ➡ Apprentice ➡ Producer ➡ Leader ➡ Mentor

A Prospect You are open minded and consider opportunities for advancement. You are dissatisfied enough to take time to learn how to improve your situation.

A Pro-sumer You are a Quixtar® cardholder. You have the right to order products at cost, register other IBOs, and sell products to customers. What you do with the opportunity can only be seen over time. An IBO who has all the right information and does nothing is basically a Pro-sumer.

An Apprentice You are an enthusiastic learner. You read books, listen to business building audios, associate with your team through seminars and strategizing sessions, show the plan, and produce product volume. With a bit of time and commitment, an apprentice will quickly become a Producer.

A Producer You have registered other IBOs and hit the 1,000 PV level on the bonus chart. You execute the five action steps - list, invite, show the plan, follow through, and repeat the process - on a consistent basis and your activity is adding IBOs to the team.

A Leader You have placed yourself a notch above the crowd. You overcome small thinking, criticism, circumstances, and obstacles that threaten to undermine the success of your team. You are a problem solver and help people focus on solutions. You breathe conviction and practice positive promotion consistently. You press on and fight for your goals and fight even harder for the people in your organization. In essence, you are a great servant to your team and are therefore trusted to lead.

You work hard, work smart, and most importantly, work in such a way that you produce results that make a difference. Your personal efforts have helped people in two or more legs hit new pin levels on the bonus chart. You've passed the acid test of leadership by creating growth from stagnation. As a leader, hitting the Platinum level and breaking Platinums in your group is only a matter of time.

A Mentor You are at the pinnacle of the leadership continuum. You have a deep sense of purpose and direction that ignites the hearts of others. You have absolute conviction, you fight for the cause, and have faith in the limitless potential of people. You develop deep-rooted relationships and build up Leaders and Mentors who carry on the cause without you.

*Note: The terms Prospect, Prosumer, Apprentice, Producer, Leader, and Mentor, used to describe the levels of leadership in this continuum are for descriptive purposes only and are not recognized by Quixtar® as achievement levels.

Regardless of where you see yourself on this leadership continuum, understand that nobody on your team wants another boss. People want to be understood first and they want to know that you have their best interest at heart. Ralph Waldo Emerson said, "Trust men and they will be true to you; treat them greatly and they will show themselves great."

Most new IBOs don't think like business owners. They don't know that it won't kill them to stay out after 10:00 pm on a weeknight. They don't know to focus on majors, not minors. They don't understand the difference between spending and investing and they don't stomach delayed gratification well. Many of them have never developed a strong work ethic or endurance. And oftentimes, they haven't had anyone ever tell them that they have what it takes. They don't know that they are capable of creating the lifestyle of their dreams.

As leaders we have to see the potential in others before they ever live up to it. And we have to walk them through the process of learning to believe it for themselves. Like a great athlete, a musician, or skilled surgeon, your leadership skills will not develop overnight. It is a journey of learning, doing, and teaching the basics over and over again. And with each new person you add to your team you strive to continually grow – that is leadership.

People are illogical, unreasonable, and self-centered.
Love them anyway.
If you do good, people will accuse you of selfish ulterior motives.
Do good anyway.
If you are successful, you win false friends and true enemies.
Succeed anyway.
The good you do today will be forgotten tomorrow.
Do good anyway.
Honesty and frankness make you vulnerable.
Be honest and frank anyway.

The biggest men and women with the biggest ideas can be shot
down by the smallest men and women with the smallest minds.
Think big anyway.
People favor underdogs but follow only top dogs.
Fight for a few underdogs anyway.
What you spend years building may be destroyed overnight.
Build anyway.
People really need help but may attack you if you do help them.
Help people anyway.
Give the world the best you have and you'll get kicked in the teeth.
Give the world the best you have anyway.

-Dr. Kent M. Keith

FIELD OF DREAMS

There once was an article about a 15-year-old kid who had dreamed his whole life of becoming a football star. He loved the game and played on his high school team, but in his junior year he started getting terrible headaches during practice. His parents grew concerned and took him to see a doctor who discovered that the boy had a brain tumor. It had progressed beyond repair and the boy was told that he would only have a few short months to live.

Despite the news, he showed up for practice that day and continued to play with the same dedication he always had. When his parents shared the news with his coach, he decided that he would play the boy as the starting quarterback at their next big game.

The day of the game, a loud parent, unhappy with the boy's performance, began yelling at the coach. "What are you doing? Get that kid out of there!" Others began chiming in with him to criticize the coach's decision until the coach, in the middle of the game,

Lead

77

walked straight up the bleachers, grabbed the parent by the scruff of the neck and said, "I don't care if we lose this game a hundred to zero, that boy is playing in this game! He's got six more weeks to live and he's living his dream tonight, don't ruin it for him."

That parent was uninvolved and had no idea what was going on. Some of you will have parents, family members, even best friends who are going to be unhappy with your decision to start a business. They may tell you, "What are you doing? Get out of there!" They may mean well, but they're most likely misinformed or uninvolved. As leaders, sometimes we feel like grabbing your biggest critics by the scruff of the neck and saying, "Look here, he's got a dream thumping in his heart and a group of people who believe in him who are helping him to live that dream. Don't ruin it, don't steal his dream from him."

As you build your business you will run into your share of people and situations that are going to attempt to ruin it all for you. Sometimes it'll be because they're uninvolved or uninformed like the loud parent at that football game; other times it'll be intentional. And the hurt and the disappointment you feel will be very real. But don't ever let that steal your wind - your dreams are worth it.

Let's face it; some people are negative about almost everything. Perhaps they "tried" something and failed and consequently have a hard time believing you, or anyone else, can succeed when they didn't. Maybe at some point they gave up on their dream and lost hope in their life so they're incapable of being hopeful for anyone else. In the worst cases, there are people who misdirect their anger and rather than using their skills and talents to improve the quality of their life, they use them to try and take everyone else down with them.

Until recently, we'd see and hear from these people on the bathroom walls and around the rumor mill, but today there is a new medium available to them: the Internet. And just about everything on the Web, including the good, the bad, and the outright lies about people and business, are now indexed by search engines. Because of the anonymity of the Web, damaging lies are now easier to tell, and it is easier to tell them without consequence.

In some cases, there is an economic motivation by the author. Perhaps the responsible party is an affiliate, a supplier of a competitor, or the competitor itself. From www.meatstinks.com (McDonald's) to www.homedepotsucks.com, www.walmartsucks. com, www.harvardsucks.com, www.fordreallysucks.com, no business is immune to it. It's just part of business and life in the information age.

There are many credible sources of facts and information available to you and your prospects to help dispel the critics like the websites www.thisbiznow.com and www.quixtarfacts.com, as well as some DVDs available directly from Quixtar®. Visit these sources to hear the other side of the story and to find out what IBOs, business executives, civic leaders, and brand experts have to say about Quixtar®. You will also discover many leading companies and brands that have chosen to affiliate themselves with Quixtar® and hear what they have to say about your business. Quixtar® is also a member of the Better Business Bureau (BBB) and the Direct Selling Association (DSA).

Lead

When I was just getting started in the business, there were people who told me that it wouldn't work, I'd never make it, I was crazy, stupid, you name it. Since I've built the business, they've stopped saying that I'd never make it; instead, they questioned where the income was really coming from along with my character, my motives, my teaching, and anything else that justified their decisions in life. It's always easier for us to point the blame at someone or something other than ourselves. I've even had people who were once close to me, maybe because they didn't appreciate my success, or for whatever reason they had, spread a bunch of negative junk about me.

As much as I've wanted everyone and everything to be the way I'd hoped they'd be, the reality of it is that life is what it is. And the only thing we have control over is our own actions and whether or not we're going to allow those disappointments to get in the way of living our dreams and helping people. It's your decision what you choose to focus on.

Before taking someone's advice ask yourself these three questions:

1. **"Do I want to live like they do?"** Their thinking got them to where they are, so it makes good sense that their thinking will get you to where they are as well. By taking their advice you will probably live very similar to how they are living.

2. **"What are they offering me?"** That is, even if your odds of success are small they are greater odds than zero. If they are not offering you any other way to achieve success, then an opportunity with proven, successful results is better than no opportunity at all.

3. "Why do I believe?" To stand your ground when you encounter someone who is critical, know why you believe. The more knowledge you have, and the clearer your vision for where you're headed, the less easily you can be influenced.

Take the information in this book, apply it, and never surrender your dream to anyone. You can do it!

Lead

RESPONSES TO QUESTIONS

"What is it?"

QUESTION: "It's _____ (your industry term), are you familiar with it?"

RESPONSE: "We have an arrangement with one of the leading shopping sites on the web, we send them customers, they send us cash." or "We teach people how to make money through a home-managed business."

FURTHER THOUGHT: If you hope to succeed in this business you should be able to answer this question in your sleep. No matter who you talk to this will be the #1 question you'll hear, so be prepared with an answer that makes sense.

"Can you tell me more about it?"

QUESTION: "Absolutely, I already have some information I can loan you. What nights this week do you already have commitments?"

RESPONSE: "Absolutely, I have an outline of the compensation plan and I'll bring it with me when I swing by." or "I'd love to go into detail, but I'm only going to confuse you. I'm calling to invite you, the meeting is set to inform you."

FURTHER THOUGHT: If someone is stuck on this question, you can give them a short, concise description of your business that peaks a person's interest. For example, "We have an arrangement with most of the fortune 500 companies where we send them customers and they send us cash. It's a brand new concept that's really growing, have you learned about it yet?" Always end with a question to regain control of the conversation.

"Is there a web site I can look at before we meet?"

QUESTION and RESPONSE: "Sure. There are plenty of web sites you can look at like Office Depot, Circuit City, and Barnes & Noble. What I'm going to show you is the profit arrangements we have with them."

"How much money are you making?"

QUESTION: "How much would you like to make?" or "Isn't it how much money you're going to make that really matters to you?"

RESPONSE: "I just started my training and expect to replace my full-time income in __ months." or "Enough to keep me interested." or "I'm just the talent scout, my senior associate is the one you want to talk to."

"Is this a pyramid?"

QUESTION: "How do you mean?" or "A pyramid?"

RESPONSE: "Of course not. Pyramids are illegal." or "Most of our partners are Fortune 500 companies. They wouldn't be associated with an illegal pyramid."

FURTHER THOUGHT: We have to understand first whether it's the structure this person is concerned about or its legality. If she's concerned about the business being structured like a pyramid, she can take a look at where she works. Is there a president, a CEO, and maybe a board of directors? Are there managers who report to them and people who report to those managers? Who makes all the money? And who really does most of the work? Do the people at the bottom all have the same opportunity to make as much money in that business as the president and CEO? What about the government? The church? Even a family has its pecking order. The difference is that in our business no one is "appointed" a position. Our compensation plan ensures the same equal opportunity for everyone and its structure is fluid. Profits are paid based on the size and number of businesses each IBO develops. In other words, we are paid on performance. Anyone has the ability to make more than the very top achiever at any time by developing a greater number of successful organizations.

"Is this Multi-level Marketing?"

QUESTION: "What's your experience with Multi-level Marketing?"

RESPONSE: "This business resembles other affiliate programs on the web. We make money by referring business." or "It's called personal franchising."

FURTHER THOUGHT: Quixtar® is actually a gigantic web of on-line affiliates who pay commissions to IBOs for their purchases and referred purchases. This type of marketing where companies pay commissions for referring business their way is called "affiliate marketing." Technically our business compensation plan is a multi-level marketing plan, but the term "multi-level" embraces too many other models that do not resemble our business in any way. Our edge is to reposition ourselves in the marketplace by drawing comparisons to other well-known companies like Visa®, American Airlines®, and Amazon.com® that participate in affiliate marketing.

"How do the product prices compare?"

QUESTION: "Compare to…?" or "Where do you shop?"

RESPONSE: "I shop regularly on the site and have found the prices to be competitive." or "They wouldn't be doing a billion dollars in sales if their prices were out of line."

"Is this Quixtar®?"

QUESTION: "What do you know about Quixtar®?" or "Are you already registered?"

RESPONSE: "Our business team_____ contracts with Quixtar® for product fulfillment, web development, and partner stores. But you will be working with me and _____, not Quixtar®."

FURTHER THOUGHT: Your answer to this question depends on their answer to your question. It would be an error to assume that the question has a negative connotation to it. The person asking this question has a perception about Quixtar® and you need to find out where he's coming from in order to respond appropriately. A similar question that you may come across is, "Is this Amway?" The i-commerce/Quixtar opportunity is not Amway. It was launched in 1999 and is a brand new business model designed specifically for the Internet. The Parent Company of Quixtar®, Alticor®, is a $4.9 billion global enterprise and parent company to many other successful companies including Quixtar®, Access Business Group, Amway®, and several others. When Quixtar® launched, it was made available to Amway distributors who chose to move to a new business. Some took advantage of the opportunity and that is why some people mistakenly lump the two separate businesses together.

HANDLING OBJECTIONS

"I'm too busy to do anything else right now."

QUESTION: "If the money was right could you find the time?" or "Would it be worth 30 minutes to find out what you're turning down?"

RESPONSE: "I know you're too busy, that's why I called you." or "Would it be worth prioritizing your time for what's important to you?" or "With your contacts and my time and experience, I think we can make some money together."

"I wouldn't be interested."

QUESTION: "How do you mean?" or "What part are you not interested in?" or "You wouldn't be interested in_____(their dream)?!?"

RESPONSE: "That's too bad, I hate to see you miss out on something this big."

FURTHER THOUGHT: It's impossible for someone not to be interested in something he hasn't even seen, so if he brings this objection up before he's seen the plan, it's most-likely a smoke-screen. A smoke-screen is someone's way of avoiding the real issue, which could be any number of things. He may not trust you, he may have come to some conclusion about the business based on your approach, he may not have a compelling reason to look at a business idea, etc. Whether he's seen the business plan or not, you'll need to find out more. What is it he's not interested in? With more specific information, you can then find a way to handle that objection by referring to the appropriate responses in this book.

"I've seen this before."

QUESTION: "What did you see?" or "Really? Tell me about it."
RESPONSE: "I had too. But I never saw it with the professional and profitable approach our team had with this industry." or "If you haven't seen it from me, you haven't seen it." or "You may have seen something like it. But if you saw what we're doing you'd be involved."

"I'm not good at sales." or "I don't like sales."

QUESTION: "What are you good at?" or "What do you like to do?" or "What is it about sales you don't like or feel that you're not good at?"
RESPONSE: "Great, that would be your first advantage."
FURTHER THOUGHT: The thought of having to "sell" turns many people off because they have a negative impression of sales due to past experiences with untrained, needy salespeople. You can relieve these fears by finding out what the person you're working with likes to do and associating that to what she would be doing in the business. If she likes to teach, we're educating people. If she enjoys friendship and community, we're making new friends. You can also emphasize the fact that we work together in teams where there is a place for everyone's unique abilities.

"I can't afford it right now."

QUESTION: "If you could afford it, would you get started right now?" or "When will you be able to afford it?" or "Why don't we start your training and you can save up the money to get started?"
RESPONSE: "You don't have to be registered to start learning about the business. If you think this is something you'd like to do, why don't we show the program to a couple of your friends? Let's take the business for a test-drive and you can get registered later." or "You've been working ___ years and you don't have $____ to your name? Don't you think it's time to change that?"

FURTHER THOUGHT: Let's face it, we always seem to find the money to do the things we want or to handle the emergencies of life. When we get a flat tire or when the fridge stops working, we figure out a way to fix it. So if someone's financial vehicle is broken, why wouldn't he do the same? What this person is really saying is that he doesn't have enough belief in his ability to succeed in the business to rearrange his financial priorities. By giving him a chance to test-drive the business, you can help increase his belief and he'll find the money.

"My spouse isn't interested."

QUESTION: "Are you interested?" or "If your spouse chose not to be involved, would you still be interested?" or "Would she support you if you chose to be involved?"

RESPONSE: "Why don't you communicate your intentions and ask her to support you?" or "Let's show her the business plan so she can make an informed decision."

FURTHER THOUGHT: To avoid this objection altogether, show the plan to both spouses at the same time. Every couple has relationship issues that come into play when making decisions so it's best that you, not a spouse, provide the information and handle the questions and objections that arise.

"I talked to a few of my friends and they're not interested."

QUESTION: "What is it they weren't interested in?" or "Does that change your desire to want to achieve your dreams?"

RESPONSE: "Tell me about your conversation." or "Of course not, you haven't been coached properly on how to talk people about this business."

"I don't know enough people."

QUESTION: "How many people do you think you'd need to know to have success?" or "If we could show you a way to find enough people, would you want this business to work for you?"

RESPONSE: "You can have great success with as few as three or four people who are interested."

FURTHER THOUGHT: This objection may mean one of several things. They may be prejudging the people they do know and what they really mean is, "I don't know enough people who would be interested." Or they may mean, "I'm uncomfortable about talking to people and am not willing to talk to enough people." Or, they may in fact know very few people. In either case, ensure them that their support team is committed to their success and prepared to walk them through the proven process of making a list and finding those who are interested.

"I don't know if I could do this."

QUESTION: "What is it you're unsure of?"

RESPONSE: "I don't know if you could either. Are you teachable? Are you motivated? Are you willing to work for what you want? If you are, then I'll help you. I think we could make a lot of money together."

FURTHER THOUGHT: Although we need to find out specifically what it is they feel they couldn't do, this objection typically boils down to a lack of belief in their ability. We want to encourage this person and let them know that anyone who is willing to learn can do this. Infuse them with your belief by making "I think" statements, getting them involved in the system, and producing results.

"I knew someone who did this and they never made any money."

QUESTION: "Really? Tell me about it."

RESPONSE: "Yeah, me too. People quit things all the time and make all kinds of excuses to justify their laziness or their lack of desire and drive. Are you like that?"

"Do I have to go to all the meetings?"

QUESTION: "What are you looking to accomplish?" or "Do you feel

you could train your business community without the meetings?"
RESPONSE: "Depends on what you want to achieve."
FURTHER THOUGHT: This person doesn't understand the value of the meetings yet because she has never had to train a community of business owners. As her business grows, however, she will begin to understand that the meetings are an efficient, timesaving way to connect with people on her team and set up meetings to work depth. Once she realizes how fun, exciting, and meaningful the meetings are, her perspective will change.

"Do I have to buy my own tools?"
QUESTION: "Do you want to buy them?"
RESPONSE: "I could loan you the tools that I've purchased and then as your business gets going, you could loan 10, 30, or 50 people the tools you've purchased and spend hundreds or thousands of dollars, or we could just all buy our own. Which makes better sense to you?"
FURTHER THOUGHT: It's one thing to loan out a few of your materials to someone new, but if you're supplying your IBOs with the tools they need to build their business, you're going to be worried about the cost of starting a new group. Not only that, when you give people tools, they won't appreciate them or take care of them as well as they would if they had to purchase them themselves.

"What are my odds of making it in this business?"
QUESTION: "What are your odds of making it without it?"
RESPONSE: "Your chances of success are the same for everyone starting this business. It's a level playing field. Your odds of success are directly related to your efforts and willingness to learn."
FURTHER THOUGHT: The person asking you this question is really asking you to tell him that you think he can do it. He's looking for encouragement, not a statistical analysis of the law of averages. In reality, odds have nothing to do with his success because his actions and decisions are not up to chance.

Q & A

"It seems like the percentage of people who make it is very low."

QUESTION: "What do you mean?" or "Why does that concern you?"

RESPONSE: Our business is structured in a way that allows everyone to do a little bit of volume, rather than a lot. In other words, if everyone is doing 100 points of volume, then for every person who achieves the level of Platinum, or 7500 points, there are 74 people who are still below the platinum level (you + 74 = 75). Divide 1 (platinum) by 75 (total people in the group) and you end up with 1.3%. Now add to that the fact that the figures are calculated based on "active" IBOs who, the corporation defines as an IBO who attempted to make a retail sale, present a business plan, or who attended a meeting or received bonus money; any one of the above. Success in the business requires much more than one attempt at anything; nevertheless, these "active" IBOs lower the averages significantly. Now, if we changed the business structure to where fewer people did more volume each, say 3000 points, then you would only need 2 people besides yourself to go platinum. Divide 1 by 3 and you get 33%, which perhaps would be a more credible percentage to someone who doesn't understand how our business works.

"Do I have to purchase 100 points of products every month?"

QUESTION: "Do you want a bonus check every month?" or "What do you want your team to duplicate?"

RESPONSE: When you become an IBO you benefit from purchasing the products you use regularly. There is no minimum and or maximum required each month. However, when you, or your customers collectively purchase 100 points of volume, you validate the compensation plan and receive a bonus check.

FURTHER THOUGHT: The person asking this question may have a concern about being forced to purchase unneeded products. Assure them that we're not looking for people to stock up on unnecessary products; we're looking for people to change the source of the products that they already use on a regular basis. Additionally, Quixtar® exclusive products have a 100% money back guarantee and are also backed by a corporate buy-back rule.

"I've always shopped at Costco, how does this business compare?"

<u>QUESTION</u>: "Does Costco® offer its shoppers the opportunity to be an equity partner?"

<u>RESPONSE</u>: It's tough to compare two companies in separate industries. Costco®, the corporation, profits from the consumer's purchases. In our business, we, the consumers, profit from our purchases.

"This would be a conflict of interest with my employer."

<u>QUESTION</u>: "How would this be a conflict?"

<u>RESPONSE</u>: "Let's find out which portion of the business is in conflict and find a way to work around it."

<u>FURTHER THOUGHT</u>: There is no doubt that some of the activities in our business could be a conflict of interest for people. Determine first if this person is looking for a solution or using this objection as an excuse. If they are sincerely looking for a solution, you can suggest putting the business in their spouse's name or refraining from business activity during working hours. There are some cases, however, where an employer will say that an employee is not allowed to pursue a secondary income because it is a conflict of interest. For an employer to take charge of all the things in your life – that's bold. They are forcing you to agree that for the fixed amount of money they give you, they control you seven days a week, twenty-four hours a day, three hundred and sixty-five days a year. They actually top you out, max you out, and make you sign your life away - and you're okay with that? What does the future hold for you if you are capped and controlled?

"I saw/read/heard this negative media piece on the business…"

QUESTION: "Tell me about what you saw/read/heard." or "Do you feel that what you saw/read/heard was a fair assessment of the business?" or "Did what you read/see/hear resemble what you've experienced?"

RESPONSE: "There are many perspectives on any issue. I think the perspective shared by hundreds of thousands of satisfied Independent Business Owners is the most compelling. I believe that you, like myself, want assurance that this business is legal, moral, ethical, and authentic. And I can, with 100% of me, say that this is a good, true, and moral endeavor. Our business system promotes men and women of integrity and character, strong families, and of course building responsible finances. I can share this opportunity with anyone and know that the business performs just as it is explained, "build a community of on-line shoppers and you will be paid for your volume."

FURTHER THOUGHT: Unfortunately, much of today's media is based on sensationalism, rather than accurate, unbiased information. Television, radio, newspaper, magazine, and other media companies are in the business of creating sensational stories that increase ratings/subscriptions in order to sell advertising. And since Quixtar® is a word of mouth business that does not purchase advertising, it becomes an easy target. It is also common for companies to spend hundreds of millions of dollars to take down their competitors, and it has been proven that some of our competitors have underhandedly done so. Directing people to the web sites www.thisbiznow.com and www.quixtarfacts.com, and/or handing them "The Facts About Quixtar®" DVD will help dispel this type of criticism.

"I heard that the leaders make all their money from the training materials."

QUESTION: "Where did you hear that?" or "Have you ever looked at the Quixtar® Bonus and Incentives brochure?"

RESPONSE: "There may be leaders out there who make a large portion of their income from the training materials, but they are the rare exception. And you'll find that happens in any industry where there are experts who, after having established their credibility through performance, will go on to make more from teaching than what they originally did. But bottom line, everyone is paid by Quixtar® based on performance. And the cash bonuses and incentives available to each and every one of us is clearly outlined in their literature. You earn it, you get it, and you can take that to the bank. So why don't we focus on which bonuses you'd like to earn this year?"

FURTHER THOUGHT: It's important that we find out from this person what their concern is first. If they are concerned that there is no income to be made in this business, other than tool income, then the response provided above should ensure them that there is a significant amount of income available to them as clearly outlined in Quixtar's literature. If, on the other hand, their concern is that they will be forced to purchase overpriced tools, you can reassure them that our training system is effective, comparatively priced, and optional. While it is highly recommended, as is training as a real estate agent, insurance agent, etc., it remains the IBO's choice whether to participate or not.

No matter how well you handle questions and objections, not everyone will get in your business. If they don't, their dream and their commitment are not as strong as yours. And that's okay. All you need is six people and they are out there waiting for you. Learn what you can from each experience, practice, get better, and go out there and find those six!

Q & A